# Imaging the Story

# Imaging the Story

*Rediscovering the Visual and Poetic Contours of Salvation*

Karen Case-Green &
Gill C. Sakakini

*with a foreword by W. David O. Taylor*

CASCADE *Books* · Eugene, Oregon

IMAGING THE STORY
Rediscovering the Visual and Poetic Contours of Salvation

Cascade Books
An Imprint of Wipf and Stock Publishers
199 W. 8th Ave., Suite 3
Eugene, OR 97401

www.wipfandstock.com

PAPERBACK ISBN: 978-1-4982-1733-0
HARDCOVER ISBN: 978-1-4982-1735-4
EBOOK ISBN: 978-1-4982-1734-7

*Cataloguing-in-Publication data:*

Names: Case-Green, Karen | Sakakini, Gill C. | Taylor, W. David O., 1972–, foreword writer

Title: Imaging the story : rediscovering the visual and poetic contours of salvation / Karen Case-Green and Gill C. Sakakini, with a foreword by W. David O. Taylor.

Description: Eugene, OR: Cascade Books, 2017 | Includes bibliographical references.

Identifiers: ISBN 978-1-4982-1733-0 (paperback) | ISBN 978-1-4982-1735-4 (hardcover) | ISBN 978-1-4982-1734-7 (ebook)

Subjects: LCSH: Christianity and art | Christian art and symbolism | Art and religion | Christianity and the arts | Aesthetics—Religious aspects—Christianity

Classification: BR115.A8 C17 2017 (print) | BR115.A8 (ebook)

Manufactured in the U.S.A.                    APRIL 27, 2017

Dedication

*For the church*

# Table of Contents

# List of Illustrations

# Foreword

Two gifts (out of many) that good artists offer their neighbors are the gift of coherence and the gift of attentiveness.

A good playwright, like Shakespeare, for example, takes the hodge-podge pieces of a family's peculiar quarrels and frames them in a coherent way. In doing this, he invites the viewer to discover a meaningful picture of what in real life is experienced as petty, maddening, and idiosyncratic, as well as perfectly predictable, while also, as often as not, dispiriting.

In the best of the bard's plays, there is no family stuff that "just" happens. There is no such thing as a stock father; there is only *this* domineering father. There is no mere mother; there is only *that* absent mother. There is no generic sister or dismissible brother; there are only *those* particular scheming siblings and *these* defiant daughters and wayward sons.

This is another way of saying that for Shakespeare there are no random families. There is only Oliver and Orlando (*As You Like It*), Goneril and Regan (*King Lear*), Katharina and Petruchio (*The Taming of The Shrew*), along with the Capulets and the Montegues (*Romeo and Juliet*). There are only these *particular* family members, with their own *raison d'être*, who are unlike any other family and yet at the same time like all families.

And it is Shakespeare's capacity to "discover" coherence in the fractured, seemingly arbitrary parts of his imagined family stories that is so deeply gratifying to us as witnesses of the plays.

Good artists, then, like novelist Zadie Smith, sculptor Henry Moore, filmmaker Kathryn Bigelow, poet Pablo Neruda, and chef Julia Child and interior designer Jean-Louis Deniot and architect Zaha Hadid and the rest, take the miscellany bits of human life and craft them in an integrated way, by all sorts of art media, to every purpose imaginable.

To witness this coherent view of life is to get a glimpse of—and in some cases to feel an intense desire for—a world made whole.

Good artists also draw our attention to things that, in some way, have become overly familiar or unseen.

In Barnett Newman's 1966 painting, "Who's Afraid of Red, Yellow and Blue," for instance, the American abstract expressionist draws the viewer's attention to *this* shade of red, positioned asymmetrically to *this* vibrant yellow, *this* "zip" of blue—not *any* red, yellow, or blue. And the meaning of these three colors is informed by a *particular* conversation unfolding in the history of modern art, not any generic conversation.

If we pay close attention, we might even hear in Newman's title the title of Edward Albee's 1962, Tony Award-winning play, *Who's Afraid of Virginia Wolf?*, which is itself a riff on the famous song from Disney's 1933 animated film, *The Three Little Pigs*, "Who's Afraid of the Big, Bad Wolf?"

So Newman's artwork is not only an invitation to attend to the nature of specific colors. It is also an invitation to attend to a specific set of fears: for abstract expressionists, the fear evoked by two world wars; for Newman, the fear of irrelevance as an artist; for Albee's characters, the fear of living an inauthentic life; and for members of the Great Depression, the fear of economic poverty.

To see Newman's painting, then, is to attend to very particular things. And in attending to these things, the hope is that the viewer will not only re-see his world but also his own life, and possibly to live anew in response to that double insight.

As it relates to the calling of Christians, philosopher Calvin Seerveld puts the point this way: "God's Spirit calls an artistic practitioner to help their neighbours who are imaginatively handicapped, who do not notice there are fifteen different greens outside their window, who have never sensed the bravery in bashfulness, or seen how lovely an ugly person can be."

For the Christian, the twin gift of coherence and attentiveness afforded by good works of art comes as welcomed news. In fact, it's nothing less than gospel stuff. It's the sort of thing, I'd hope, that we ought to be making and promoting and patronizing ourselves. And, in a sense, this is exactly what Gill and Karen offer the reader in their book, *Imaging the Story*.

They take the Scriptures as their frame and invite the reader to perceive a coherent story told from start to finish. All things—all the bits and bobs of history, the quirks of human beings, the quarrels of civilizations, the eccentricities of places, all the tragic events and the ineffable moments of wonder and the tremors of nature, all products of human design and divine imagination—find their proper meaning in this particular story.

Colossians 1:17 says that in Christ, the firstborn of creation, "all things *hold together.*" This is another way of saying that in Christ all things cohere; not just some things or the good things, but *all* things. Likewise, as Saint John reminds us, Christ is the very light of the world. By his light all things are rightly seen. All things are carefully attended to. All things, in all their quiddity, are beheld in love.

And so it is "meet and right," to use the language of the *Book of Common Prayer*, that Gill and Karen take the grand narrative of Scripture as their starting point. To see the "big picture," as they tell it, is to see one's place in that picture. And when you and I discover how we fit into that picture, we begin to discover a way to receive care and to give care.

For readers of this book, my hope is that you will find your calling as a Christian and as an artist fully affirmed. My hope is that the artistic exercises that accompany each chapter will strengthen muscles to take on your creative projects with new resolve. My hope is that the practice of *Lectio Divina* will speak peace to your soul and that the exposure to works of visual art and poetry will inspire you and remind you that you are not alone.

As we see repeatedly in this lovely book, a great cloud of witnesses has gone before us and testify—knowingly in some cases, unknowingly in others—to the good work of God in the world. As you find your place in this cloud of witnesses, my prayer is that you will be encouraged to make your own work, work that draws our attention to things as-yet not fully seen and to the kind of wholeness for which the human heart deeply yearns.

W. David O. Taylor

Assistant Professor of Theology & Culture,
Fuller Theological Seminary

# Introduction

## Soaring to see

God's story intersects with our story. The grand metanarrative, which runs throughout the Bible, also weaves in and out of particular individuals' lives and the lives of particular communities. However, it is easy to lose sight of the big story. Caught up in our own individual dramas, our eyes shift from the overarching drama and we quickly lose perspective.

Of all the Gospel writers, the apostle John keeps his sights—and ours—trained on the big story.[1] When Jesus bids farewell to his disciples before his death, John includes a speech in which Jesus reminds his disciples that their sorrow, like the pain of a woman in labor, will pass and will one day be turned to great joy (John 16:21–22). They are encouraged to look up and look ahead to the big story. Such vision keeps hope alive.

Over the years, John came to be represented by the image of an eagle in some church traditions due to the way he seems to soar the highest and see the furthest. This book invites you to take this eagle's view on the story.

## Imagery, imagination, . . . and the Bible

You might be asking, "Why 'imaging the story'?" While we are grateful for the many courses that have helped us to engage with the salvation story through discussion and analysis, we feel there is a need to engage our *imaginations* with the story and to make things in creative response to it. Paul writes to the church in Ephesus, "For we are God's handiwork, created in Christ Jesus to do good works, which God prepared in advance for us to do" (Eph 2:10 NIV). The Greek word *poieō*, from which we get the word

---

1. We are grateful to Philip Greenslade for his book *The Big Story,* which charts a journey through the overarching salvation narrative.

"workmanship" (*poiēma*), means "to make."[2] It does not just mean "to do good deeds." As we shall see in chapter 1, when God made things he made them beautiful as well as good.

One summer, my family and I (Karen) followed the river Dee as we walked in Snowdonia and later travelled by narrow boat. We watched the river grow as it journeyed through Wales and into England, towards the sea. Crossing and re-crossing it on our narrow boat, we made the spectacular journey across the Pontycysyllte Aqueduct. When we arrived at our final destination, we walked along the riverside, admiring the power and vitality of this magnificent river. Noticing a church on the bank, I approached it, wanting somewhere to give thanks. However, when I drew near I found high bars fronting the church and a meager, lack-luster sign pinned to them. The contrast between the river to my right and the church to my left could not have been starker. The sign may just as well have read, "Beauty—keep out."

For many years, the church lost its ability to respond visually to the salvation story. This was due, in part, to the Protestant Reformation, which tended to prioritize word over image. It treated the visual imagination like an embarrassing elderly relative, to be kept away at all costs from the things of faith that mattered. There were good reasons for this suspicion for, as we shall see in chapter 2, images can fast become idols.

Yet the Bible is image-rich. Most biblical writers are fluent in both the verbal and the visual languages, perhaps none more so than the apostle John. As well as being known for his eagle's perspective, John is also celebrated as something of an artist. From the start of his gospel, word and image go hand in hand. John is not alone in this. As the Scottish theologian and minister, John McIntyre, points out, the parables, poetry, and apocalypses in the Bible all depend on images and on the imagination that creates them.[3] These art forms help us to imagine the world differently; they re-vision things.

Our desire is to engage your imaginations in the salvation story. Poetry, stories, and visual art do not need to lead us away from truth; they can, in fact, in the words of Emily Dickinson, "Tell all the truth but tell it slant."[4] Like John the artist and many prophet-poets in the Bible, we wish to

---

2. Brown and Loades, *Christ: The Sacramental Word*, 3.

3. McIntyre, *Faith, Theology and Imagination*, 3.

4. Dickinson, *The Collected Poems of Emily Dickinson*.

help you behold—to stop and see the story through fresh eyes—and later to tell it yourselves through what you make.

Some people may feel that the arts are exclusive and only to be enjoyed by a privileged few. However, we believe that we are made in the image of a creator God who has imparted his creative DNA to us. Creativity is not elitist because God is not elitist. Another hang-up some people have is that "making" is something we usually leave behind in the classroom. As one of Britain's best-loved illustrators, Quentin Blake, reminds us, "We start life with the possibility of two languages, verbal and visual";[5] and, while we tend to be fluent in both these languages as children, many of us grow distant from visual language as we grow older. We may consider it childish. Perhaps we have something to learn from G. K. Chesterton here:

> It is possible that God says every morning, "Do it again," to the sun; and every evening, "Do it again," to the moon. It may not be automatic necessity that makes all daisies alike: it may be that God makes every daisy separately, but has never got tired of making them. It may be that He has the eternal appetite of infancy; for we have sinned and grown old, and our Father is younger than we.[6]

God is a maker, as we shall see in chapter 1, and we are made in his image. This course invites you to re-discover this "eternal appetite of infancy" and to share in his joy of making.

## Curating the soul

Before we make anything we will stop and behold—reading God's word and reflecting on the visual and verbal art that has been made in response to it. The opportunity to "behold" is actually a profound act of self-care. When Jesus said, "Love your neighbor as you love yourself" (Matt 22:39), the premise was that loving yourself sets the standard for loving others. One of the driving forces behind this book is the need for greater soul-care. In danger of being driven by the "tyranny of the urgent,"[7] perhaps nowhere more so than in the church, the real challenge is to find pools of stillness and refreshment within the sometimes humdrum, sometimes frenetic, routine of our everyday lives.

---

5. Blake, "Drawn into a Parallel World," R28.

6. Chesterton, *Orthodoxy*, 58.

7. Stackhouse, *The Day is Yours*, 59.

We are certainly not called to avoid activity. Indeed, Christ calls us into active participation in his kingdom purposes. The last thing we want to encourage through this course is the spawning of a group of "artists," living in splendid isolation. Instead, we wish to follow the monastic approach to solitude, which has been defined as "a healthy turning toward one's beloved."[8] By using art and poetry to help us reflect, we will create still points where you can be drawn into the divine circle of love between Father, Son, and Spirit, a love that then goes out into the world.

**Figure 01:** *The Icon of the Trinity* **by Andrei Rublev, fifteenth century, Tretyakov Gallery, Moscow (142 cm × 114 cm)**[9]

8. Dubay, *Fire Within*, 122.

9. The Father is seated on the left, the Spirit on the right, and the Son in the center (with the tree, foreshadowing the cross, behind him). This piece is also known as "The Hospitality of Abraham."

Rublev's icon of the Trinity invites us to participate in this creative life of the Godhead. While the icon depicts the three visitors to Abraham (Gen 18), on another level it evokes the persons of the Trinity and shows their dynamic relationship. Each figure inclines towards the other and honors their presence in a never-ending circle. In the center is the cup, so central to the salvation story, and a reminder of the missional impulse at the heart of the Trinity. In the foreground is a place for us to take, if we wish to participate.

## Following the contours of the story

Rublev's icon reminds us that "God mediates himself to the world through the Son."[10] The biblical story is Christocentric; Christ stands at the *center* of it. Nowhere is the intersection of God's story and ours seen more sharply than in Christ's coming. This book will follow the contours of the salvation story, building up to the climax of Jesus' coming to earth, and leading away from that. We will follow the narrative thread from the creation of the world in chapter 1, through to the promised consummation in chapter 10 when Jesus returns. And we shall be adopting John's eagle-eye perspective as we track the story from start to finish.

Following the contours of the story will take us to some tortuous places. In chapter 2 we respond to the crisis that erupts when humankind rebels against God. However, chapter 3 sounds a note of hope as we hear the calling of Abram and consider our own calling into God's redemptive plans. Mary's conception is celebrated in chapter 4, along with the chance to add our creative "Yes" to her own voice. But at the center of the story is Jesus, so the chapters that follow explore Christ's coming (chapter 5), cross and comeback (chapter 6); while chapter 7 looks at the gifts imparted to the disciples through the Holy Spirit. The new fledgling community, the church, formed as a result of Christ's death and resurrection, are explored in chapters 8 and 9. The story closes in chapter 10 with a celebration of the new heaven and earth, where face-to-face seeing is restored.

## How to navigate this book

Each chapter will guide you through the following activities:

10. Tomlin, *The Widening Circle*, 15.

1. *Read* the biblical text.

2. *Respond.* This will be a chance to engage with the text through questions. *Visuo divina* ("divine seeing") can also be used to help you deepen your understanding of the passage.

3. *Reflect.* We want to create time and space for you to be gathered into God's story, not just through your head, but also through your imagination. To that end, the biblical text will be put in conversation with visual art and poetry in each chapter.

4. *Make.* Each chapter gives you the opportunity to playfully participate in the story by creating something—either visual or verbal—in response to the particular theme of the chapter.

You can read this coursebook on your own, but it works best if you are also part of a group with whom you meet regularly to discuss the chapters and to make things. You will need to read the chapter before you meet and the group sessions will work best if you have done any activities outlined in the chapter beforehand. Those activities to be done as a group will be highlighted in the chapter. Meeting up with your group can be a good time to discuss and share your work so far and to "sharpen" each other (Prov 27:17).

## Posturing yourself

One of the most important ways in which art can act upon us is by creating a sense of naked humility. According to C. S. Lewis, "The first demand of any work of art is surrender. Look. Listen. Receive. Get yourself out of the way."[11] There is no room for pride here: you and I will bring our own thread of color to the salvation story, but ultimately this is not "my story" but "his story." So it is good to have the right posture before we enter the story. Before you begin the course, we'd encourage you to take time to do the following activity.

In the crypt of Winchester Cathedral stands a life-size statue of a man. This sculpture by Antony Gormley is called *Sound II.* As the crypt floods regularly during the winter months, the man is often surrounded by water. As he cups his hands and looks down, surrounded by the reflective water,

---

11. Lewis, "An Experiment in Criticism," 18–19.

he seems to be taking a sounding of himself.[12] Look at the image and then read the poem below by Jan Richardson to posture yourself at the start of this course.

**Figure 02:** *Sound II* **by Antony Gormley, Winchester Cathedral, Winchester**

**Stay**

I know how your mind
rushes ahead,
trying to fathom
what could follow this.
What will you do,
where will you go,
how will you live?

You will want
to outrun the grief.
You will want

12. A nautical term which refers to the process to determine a water's depth, either under a ship or in a tank.

to keep turning toward
the horizon,
watching for what was lost
to come back,
to return to you
and never leave again.

For now,
hear me when I say
all you need to do
is to still yourself,
is to turn toward one another,
is to stay.

Wait
and see what comes
to fill
the gaping hole
in your chest.
Wait with your hands open
to receive what could never come
except to what is empty
and hollow.

You cannot know it now,
cannot even imagine
what lies ahead,
but I tell you
the day is coming
when breath will
fill your lungs
as it never has before,
and with your own ears
you will hear words
coming to you new
and startling.

You will dream dreams
and you will see the world
ablaze with blessing.

Wait for it.
Still yourself.
Stay.[13]

## Reflect

1. Look at the man's posture in *Sound II*. What kind of attitude does it suggest?

2. The poet tells us to, "Wait with your hands open/ to receive what could never come." Cup your own hands before God at the start of this course.

3. Be aware of your body as you "still yourself."

4. Ask God to take a "sounding" of your own life. You might like to use these words as a prayer to ask God to sound you out:

   Search me, O God, and know my heart;
   test me and know my thoughts.
   (Ps 139:23)

5. Ask God's Spirit to help you surrender to him as you enter the story.

You might like to return to the poem and Gormley's sculpture as a way of getting into position at the start of each chapter.

---

13. Richardson, *Circle of Grace*, 161. "Stay" © Jan Richardson from *Circle of Grace: A Book of Blessings for the Seasons*.

## chapter 1

# Creation

## Creator and Craftsman

The story starts here. In Genesis 1, the writer soars up high to give us a cosmic overview of creation. Little detail is given as to how or when creation occurs; what is important to the writer is *who* is behind it. As the story opens, God is depicted as the divine protagonist.[1]

In this grand choreography, *'Elohim* (the generic Hebrew term for God) is seen at a lofty distance, summoning life through the "mere agency of divine speech."[2] He creates *ex nihilo* (creating things out of nothing), simply by speaking things into being. The Hebrew verb *bara'* in Genesis 1 is used to describe the way in which God creates and, occurring fifty times in the Old Testament, God is the only subject of this verb. Human beings cannot create like this; it is sole territory of the divine.

Simple though the first creation account may seem, it is tightly crafted. Enclosed within an envelope structure, strong word patterns emerge.[3] For instance, we read that, after God creates each thing, he declares that, "it was good." This phrase acts like a refrain throughout Genesis 1. The English translation "good" fails to capture the richness of this word. The Hebrew term, *tov,* is highly nuanced and suggests "beautiful," "delightful," "prosperous," and "working the way it was created to," as well as meaning "morally

---

1. We see the Trinity present in creation, with God's Spirit hovering over the waters and his Word present as the active agent.

2. Altar, *The Five Books of Moses,* 20.

3. Alter suggests that Gen 2:1–4 echoes Gen 1:1. Ibid., 20–21.

good." So land, plants, trees, sun, moon, and every kind of creature on and above the earth are all declared *tov* and are blessed by God. Everything works the way it was created to work and is a good thing to behold.

In Genesis 2, the focus changes. From the grand choreography of Genesis 1, we swoop down suddenly to earth and see God working as a craftsman, forming and shaping out of the superabundance of creation. The verb *yatsar* (fashioning) replaces *bara'* (creating) to describe the Creator at work, forming the human (*'adam*) from the soil (*'adamah*), blowing life into his nostrils (Gen 2:7), building woman from his rib (Gen 2:22), and planting a garden (Gen 2:8).[4] In short, we are plunged into the nitty-gritty of "making."

## Read

Read the passage below slowly. [5]

> In the day that the Lord God made the earth and the heavens, when no plant of the field was yet in the earth and no herb of the field had yet sprung up—for the Lord God had not caused it to rain upon the earth, and there was no one to till the ground, but a stream would rise from the earth, and water the whole face of the ground—then the Lord formed man from the dust of the ground, and breathed into his nostrils the breath of life; and the man became a living thing. And the LORD God planted a garden in Eden, in the east; and there he put the man whom he had formed. Out of the ground the LORD God made to grow every tree that is pleasant to the sight and good for food, the tree of life also in the midst of the garden, and the tree of the knowledge of good and evil.
>
> A river flows out of Eden to water the garden, and from there it divides and becomes four branches. The name of the first is Pishon; it is the one that flows around the whole land of Havilah, where there is gold; and the gold of that land is good; bdellium and onyx stone are there. The name of the second river is Gihon; it is the one that flows around the whole land of Cush. The name of the third river is Tigris, which flows east of Assyria. And the fourth river is the Euphrates.
>
> The LORD God took the man and put him in the garden of Eden to till it and keep it. . . . Then the LORD God said, "It is not

4. Ibid.

5. We'd invite you to use *visuo divina* to read this text. See Appendix 1 for instructions. Feel free to use this approach to the biblical texts in each chapter.

good that the man should be alone; I will make him a helper as his partner." So out of the ground the LORD God formed every animal of the field and every bird of the air, and brought them to the man to see what he would call them; and whatever the man called each living creature, that was its name. The man gave names to all cattle, and to the birds of the air, and to every animal of the field . . . . (Gen 2:4–20)

## Respond

- What do you notice about the nitty-gritty of making in the text above?
- How are Adam and Eve invited to be co-makers with God in the garden?

Figure 03: *The Awakening Slave*
by Michelangelo, c. 1520–23, Galleria dell'Accademia, Florence

**Figure 04: *The Hand of God***
**by Auguste Rodin, 1896, Rodin Museum, Paris**

## Reflect

- Compare these two sculptures. How does each artist seem to work with the material?

- Which creation account (Genesis 1 or 2) does each artist seem to reflect?

- Which way of working do you identify with most?

Michelangelo's work is one of four unfinished sculptures of captives. In this one, a figure emerges from a huge marble block. It evokes the idea that making art is about discovering the potential lying within a given material, and drawing it out. In this way it reminds us of Genesis 2, in that all the necessary materials have been provided in creation for artistic endeavours. Hierarchically speaking, the actual substance of the earth (marble) is formed at creation, and humankind—subsequently formed *"from the dust of the ground*" (Gen 2:7)—can *act* on the stone or marble, causing it to reveal its hidden potential and *telos* (purpose). The artist is invited to delve, mine, and seek out the myriad resources from which human creation takes place. Compared with Rodin's sculpture, the absence of a hand in Michelangelo's work may also suggest that God's word alone is sufficient for the creative act to occur.

This approach to his material greatly informed Michelangelo's work. Story has it that one day he was seen sweating as he manoeuvred a large rock down the street. An onlooker, standing idly at a doorway, asked why on earth he was expending so much effort in shifting a lump of stone. "Because," came the reply, "there's an angel in there that wants to walk free."[6]

Auguste Rodin's sculpture *The Hand of God* depicts the way in which God acts on the material to create humankind. God's large right hand cradles a natural, grainy lump of marble, and we see how he creates by modelling and shaping the figures of Adam and Eve, rather than excavating them from the clay. The limbs are built up as pressure acts on the malleable earth. The similarity of God's hand to the human flesh may strike some as audacious but can be read symbolically to indicate that we are made in God's own image—"Let us make humankind in our image, according to our likeness" (Gen 1:26)—and can therefore create like him, although not, of course, from nothing.

## Reflect

- What new insights might these sculptures contribute to your understanding of Genesis 2?
- What do they suggest about "making" and/or "being made"?

## A dynamic gift

The materiality of creation is celebrated in Genesis 2 as gift in the fact that God does not just give us "nature," he gives us *cultivated* nature; he plants a garden! What does this say about the way we were made to live? The garden in Eden is a place to be fashioned and designed, using the raw materials. It is not a static, finished product; it is a *dynamic gift*. Humans are given the opportunity to garden and tend; both are verbs that describe the active

6. Dewar, *Invitations,* 34.

shaping and ordering of a given piece of earth, as well as the nurturing of life.

In addition to the obvious vegetation and flora, the Garden of Eden contains hidden substances below the surface identified as gold, bdellium, and onyx, all of which evoke rich color and extravagance (Gen 2:11–12). Interestingly, there is no mention of the presence of chalk, iron, and granite, good and functional though these things are. Instead, we find minerals of sheer beauty, placed out of sight, waiting to be mined. The latent potential within each mineral, metal, or piece of earth waits to be realized by humankind. This will be an important theme in chapter 3 as we consider our vocation as "makers." Once discovered, the human delight in making can be fulfilled in that these beautiful materials are prime for shaping, molding, and fashioning into functional vessels, certainly, but also into artworks of utter beauty with no prescribed use whatsoever.

## Just because

**Figure 05: Image from Lascaux Caves, France**

In 1940, four teenagers stumbled upon a cave in southwest France. Upon entering, they discovered it to be teeming with visual life: images of horses, stags, cattle, bison—as well as abstract signs—lined the cave walls. The Palaeolithic paintings at the cave complex of Lascaux are now world-famous, and are a visual celebration of the sheer abundance and diversity of living creatures. These creatures are depicted with haunting grace and beauty, and there is something utterly gratuitous about the wealth of images on the walls.[7]

Why, you might ask, when prehistoric humans had more pressing things on their minds (like survival), did they waste time painting images of creatures, some of which were of no utilitarian value to them whatsoever?[8] Perhaps this urge to make, not only for utilitarian purposes but also for the *sheer delight of making* ("just because . . ."), is universal and has its ontological roots in the creation story in Genesis. Made in God's image, the creative impulse we experience is God's own creative pulse in us.[9] What if, in the act of making, whether it be cave paintings, buildings, gardens, or poems, we are actually imaging something of our Creator?

As we grow older, many of us stop making things, even if we enjoyed doing so in our youth. With so many other pressing needs, it seems indulgent, even wasteful, to "make" simply for the sake of it. However, according to the passage above, the trees that God plants in the Garden of Eden are not just utilitarian—good *for* something (food)—they are also "good to the eye" (Gen 2:9). They are *beautiful*. This suggests that aesthetics matter, as well as functionality, to the eye of this divine designer.

There was a time when the church placed equal value on God's truth, goodness, and beauty in theology. However, the balance got lost over time, with different church traditions emphasizing one aspect of the triangle at the expense of another. Today many churches emphasize the *true* (in their focus on God's word) and are showing a growing commitment to the *good* (in their increased awareness of ethical trading, support of Stop the Traffic and other justice-seeking initiatives); however, *beauty* has often been like Cinderella at the ball. One of the aims of this book is to re-engage churches with God's delight in beauty, while holding fast to his truth and goodness. To enjoy making, just because. . . .

7. Over nine hundred images of animals have been identified.

8. While some of the creatures would have been sources of food and others were predators to be feared, this does not account for the sheer wealth of images on the walls and the presence of animals that were of no particular "use."

9. A theme that Rob Bell develops well in his seminar, "Beginning in the Beginning" on the *Poets, Prophets, and Preachers* DVD.

## Make

This activity is to be done in a group. Your leader will provide you with the necessary materials.

### A. Attending and drawing

Spend some time looking attentively at natural objects that you come across in everyday life. Choose several, hold them and note your responses to their character. Make loose sketches and, as you do so, be aware of the texture, shape, and tone of the object, or where it may have come from. What are its distinctive features? How do the marks you make capture what you see? Are any memories evoked as you make this visual exploration? Invite your senses into this sketching process as you focus on and follow the contours of this shape.

### B. Seeing the form

During the last decade of his life when his eyesight deteriorated, the artist Henri Matisse came to see and create form in a fresh way—through cutting out shapes of things he saw around him from painted paper. As he incised into brightly colored papers, the very process of cutting out caused the image to be simplified to its core. In what have become known as the "cut-outs," the essence of the object is crystallized by the artist into the barest form, yet no vitality is compromised. The opposite is in fact true, for as the shapes are pared down life teams from his compositions.

Look up Matisse's cutouts online. E.g. *La Treatise du Roi* or *Polynesia, the Sea.*

### C. Re-drawing and painting

From your loose sketches now draw images that simplify one object and tighten up the details. Consider what essence you can distill from your object and decide how to emphasize its particularity by exaggerating certain features or patterns. Next, using acrylic paints, transfer your designs onto two white tiles. When the paint is dry, paint a layer of clear varnish over the face of the tiles and leave to dry.

Figure 06: Tile-painting during Lent course, 2014, Fox's Barn

## Digging for names

In Genesis 2, we witness a celebration of verbal, as well as visual, language as God invites Adam to participate in his creative project by naming the creatures. We read that "out of the ground the LORD God formed every animal of the field and every bird of the air, and brought them to the man to see what he would call them; and whatever the man called each living creature, that was its name" (Gen 2:19).

Understated and matter-of-fact though this verse may seem, the implications are in fact quite staggering. There is something very significant about naming. It can capture the identity of a person or thing due to the paramount relationship that seems to exist between the essence of a thing and its representation.[10] Conversely, some names seem absurd because they fail to spell out what Hopkins calls the "this-ness" of a creature. For instance, while cycling across our local common to catch a train one day, I (Karen) was set upon by a small but rather determined terrier. She kept up with my bike effortlessly and was still left with enough breath to yap and snap at my heels. As I tried unsuccessfully to shake her off, a large man came running over the brow of the hill bellowing, "Thumbelina!" The name

10. Freedman, *Emily Dickinson and the Religious Imagination,* 54.

may have suited the sweet puppy she no doubt once was, but it did not fit the aggressive creature trying to lock its jaws around my left foot!

Names matter. How many parents have agonized over what names to give their babies and have postponed the naming until after the child is born? We feel the weight of responsibility because we are aware that, to some degree, the name will represent the person, as we shall see in chapter 7.

Yet God invites Adam to *name* the animals that he has made. What a privilege. What a risk! Just picture it now: after creating, forming, and shaping each creature—with all the artistic autonomy that this requires—the Lord brings them before Adam and allows him to put his own creative stamp on their final identities. Why would God do this, but for his wish to share in the delight and playfulness of "making" with us?

God allows Adam to put his own creative seal on each creature—there is finality to it: "and whatever the man called each living creature, that was its name" (Gen 2:19). Being given the unique privilege of naming other creatures shows how, as Philip Greenslade puts it, "human beings share God's authority to define the world."[11] There is no dislocation between word and thing in Eden while it is in this state of wholeness and peace (*shalom*), and Adam is invited to put his own mark on each creature's identity by naming it.

Seamus Heaney finishes his poem, "Digging," with these lines: "Between my finger and my thumb/ the squat pen rests/ I'll dig with it." Writing can be a kind of "digging," whether it's prose, poems, or songs: a mining of the wonders of creation that lie just beneath the surface.

You are now going to read a poem that celebrates our freedom to name things in creation with exuberant playfulness. The poet captures something of the essence, or "thisness," of a created thing. This extract comes from Seamus Heaney's translation of a poem that plays with the names of the hare.

> The hare, call him scotart,
> big-fellow, bouchart,
> the O'Hare, the jumper,
> the rascal, the racer . . . .
> The wimount, the messer,
> the skidaddler, the nibbler,

11. Greenslade, *The Big Story*, 98.

the ill-met, the slabber.
The quick-scut, the dew-flirt,
the grass-biter, the goibert,
the home-late, the do-the-dirt.
The starer, the wood-cat,
the purblind, the furze cat,
the skulker, the bleary-eyed,
the wall-eyed, the glance-aside
and also the hedge-springer.
The stubble-stag, the long lugs,
the stook-deer, the frisky legs,
the wild one, the skipper,
the hug-the-ground, the lurker,
the race-the-wind, the skiver,
the shag-the-hare, the hedge-squatter,
the dew-hammer, the dew-hopper,
the sit-tight, the grass-bounder,
the jig-foot, the earth-sitter,
the light-foot, the fern-sitter,
the kail-stag, the herb-cropper.
The creep-along, the sitter-still,
the pintail, the ring-the-hill,
the sudden start,
the shake-the-heart,
the belly-white,
the lambs-in-flight . . . .[12]

## Reflect

Read through and highlight your favorite names for the hare. How does the poem capture different aspects of this creature?

12. Extract from Heaney's "The Names of the Hare." Translation of anonymous Middle English lyric. Faber and Faber Ltd. Used by permission.

## Make

We'd encourage you to do this activity on your own and then to share it with your group when you meet.

1. Think of a creature that you would like to celebrate through words. What does it look like? What does it do? How does it move? Jot some ideas down to capture its essence—try to stay particular and "earthy." Don't worry about the order or whether you think the words are any good at this stage. Just write.

2. Now turn those words into a list of names. Turn adjectives into nouns. E.g.,

| "He has frisky legs" | — | "the frisky legs" |
| "he has a white belly" | — | "the belly-white" |
| (adjective) | | (noun) |

3. Finally, read your list aloud and play around with the order of the names. Which ones sound good together? (E.g., "the belly-white,/ the lambs-in-flight")

Making something and then setting it free is to share in something of our Creator's own respect for what he makes. If God allows his creation to be enjoyed—and interpreted—by others, then we too can set what we make free (be they poems, paintings, sculptures, children, sermons) for others to receive, or reject, as they will. This may seem a risk, but it is one our Creator took long ago!

This making is not limited to poetry. It includes a breadth of creative activity, defined by taking up the raw materials of creation and responding to the God-given instinct to make and to share in God's creative purposes in the world. This is a privilege we wish to explore with you as we journey together through God's story.

You might want to make this poem by Ann Lewin something of a prayer at the start of this course:

## Revelation

God's work of art.
That's me?
Then beauty must lie

In the eye of the
Beholder.
I feel more like
One of those statues
Michelangelo left
Half emerging
From the marble block;
Full of potential,
On the verge of life,
But prisoned still
By circumstance and
Fear.
Yet part of me is free—
And you are still creating,
Bringing to life
The promise that is there.
Sometimes by
Hammer blows
Which jar my being,
Sometimes by
Tender strokes half felt
Which waken me to
Life.
Go on, Lord.
Love me into wholeness.
Set me free
To share with you
In your creative joy;
To laugh with you
At your delight
In me,
Your work of art.[13]

---

13. "Revelation" from *Watching for the Kingfisher* by Ann Lewin, published by Canterbury Press. © Ann Lewin 2004, 2006, and 2009. Used by permission.

## chapter 2

# Crisis

## God's "Yes"

In the last chapter we explored how God's first word to Adam was a huge, divine "Yes" to abundant life. The garden contained all that was good for food but also good to the eye—it was aesthetically beautiful. It was all *"tov."*

This was a safe place for relationships. Against the backdrop of the garden, a human community of trust and well-being could flourish.[1] Perhaps nowhere was God's abundant "Yes" more evident than in the creation of Eve herself. With her beside him, Adam could now enjoy communion with God and with his fellow human beings, in perfect *shalom.*

### Reflect

Look at your tile(s). Give thanks for the abundant beauty, color, and life that God created at the beginning.

## Dis-ease

Today, many would consider it naïve of artists to celebrate the world's beauty. Indeed, the shalom of the garden has become a distant echo and beauty a dirty word to many in the contemporary art world. Recent art movements have almost outdone themselves to express the *un-tov* over the last century,

1. Brueggemann, *Genesis*, 47.

and some of these works have become highly prized. For example, in May 2012, Edvard Munch's painting *The Scream* set a world record when it was sold at auction for $119,922,500. Painted in 1893, Munch's vision seems to have a prescient quality, given the devastation that humans went on to inflict upon each other in the following century. The painting touches a universal nerve in expressing a sense of "dis-ease."

**Figure 07:** *The Scream*
**by Edvard Munch, 1893, National Gallery, Oslo (91 cm x 73.5 cm)**

The well-being, or *shalom,* that existed in the garden between Adam and Eve and between them and God is shattered by the end of Genesis 3.

## Reflect

Can you think of any other visual art that represents human "dis-ease"?

## The serpent in the tale

As we saw in chapter 1, the garden was "good" *(tov)* in every sense of the word. It had everything that Adam and Eve could wish for in terms of food, beauty, companionship, and fulfillment. But now, instead of letting God decide what is "good," they start to judge for themselves.

## Read

Read the passage below slowly.

> Now the serpent was more crafty than any other wild animal that the LORD God had made. He said to the woman, "Did God say, 'You shall not eat from any tree in the garden'?" The woman said to the serpent, "We may eat of the fruit of the trees in the garden; but God said, 'You shall not eat of the fruit of the tree that is in the middle of the garden, nor shall you touch it, or you shall die.'" But the serpent said to the woman, "You will not die; for God knows that when you eat of it your eyes will be opened, and you will be like God, knowing good and evil." So when the woman saw that the tree was good for food, and that it was a delight to the eyes, and that the tree was to be desired to make one wise, she took of its fruit and ate; and she also gave some to her husband, who was with her, and he ate. Then the eyes of both were opened, and they knew that they were naked; and they sewed fig leaves together and made loincloths for themselves.
>
> They heard the sound of the LORD God walking in the garden at the time of the evening breeze, and the man and his wife hid themselves from the presence of the Lord God among the trees of the garden. (Gen 3: 1–24)

## Respond

- Which words or images lingered with you as you read the passage?
- The tale is economically told. What did you notice about the details that *were* included?

What happens to Eve's "seeing" in the text is significant. In verse 6 we read that "the woman saw that the tree was good for food, and that it was a delight to the eyes, and that the tree was to be desired to make one wise."

There seems to be a tragic echo of Genesis 2 in these words. When God made the garden, he ensured that there were all kinds of trees—trees that were "pleasant to the sight and good for food" (Gen 2:4–9). Throughout Genesis 1, we hear this refrain seven times: "And God saw that it was good." Then we are told that, after making mankind, God surveys all that he has made and pronounces it "very good." Now, the God who had spoken his divine "Yes" over human life, and whose "No" had only existed to protect that life, will be referred to by Eve only in terms of his prohibition.[2] Eve will now use her own eyes to judge what is good—and looking will soon grow to lusting. The Hebrew *ta'avah* in verse 6 means "that which is intensely desired" and it relates to appetite. Eve has hungry eyes. And so she eats, and Adam eats.

## Make

According to Brueggemann, three things that God gave Adam and Eve in the garden get distorted in the dialogue between the serpent and Eve: first, the vocation (as creative co-workers); second, the permission (concerning what *can* be eaten in the garden); and third, the prohibition (concerning what *cannot* be eaten).[3]

*The following activity is to be done in the group session.*

1. First, compare what God *actually* says in Genesis 2:15–25 with what the serpent and Eve say he says in Genesis 3.[4]

2. How do God's words get twisted?

3. Take long strips of paper—colored or white. Write one of God's "vocation," "permission," or "prohibition" statements found in Genesis 2:15–17. Think about how you might show the good intended by God through the way you write your text and your choice of color. You could continue this process with other statements if you wish.

4. Next, tightly coil the strips so that they will twist as they unfurl.

2. Ibid., 48.

3. Ibid., 53.

4. For example, God says in Genesis 2:16, "You may freely eat of every tree of the garden; but of the tree of the knowledge of good and evil you shall not eat, for in the day that you eat of it you shall die." However, the serpent exaggerates the command—"Did God say, 'You shall not eat from any tree in the garden'?" (Gen 3:1).

5. You might like to hang the twisted strips together.

6. Reflect on the word-twisting that still happens in our world today.

## From dust you came

The serpent tricks Eve into thinking she can play God. She starts treating God's word arrogantly, as if she has the right to judge it for herself. She doesn't—she's come from 'Adam: the Hebrew name shares its root with the word 'adamah, meaning "humus," or "earth."[5] Eve is an *earthling*.

We are earthlings too. From dust we came and to dust we will return. The word "humus" is also linked to the word "humble." The soil that God wants to cultivate in our hearts is the soil of humility and the seeds of our "making," which will be explored in the next two chapters, need this soil in which to grow and flourish.

Interestingly, Satan is never once mentioned in this story. Not until the New Testament is the serpent in Eden directly identified with the devil.[6] All we know from Genesis is that "the serpent was more crafty than any other wild animal that the LORD God had made." Perhaps this is because it is essentially *our* story that is being told. As Jacobs suggests:

> To know our own condition is vital; to know that of other creatures is not. How Adam and Eve moved from rebellion we must understand; how Satan and his allies made the same move is a matter of indifference. . . . The story of original sin . . . is our story.[7]

## Over-exposure

What happens next is the stuff of nightmares. "Then the eyes of both were opened, and they knew that they were naked" (Gen 3:7). Being naked in your dreams is often interpreted as feeling exposed. Eve and Adam had wanted knowledge and knowledge is what they get: they know more than they wanted and now there is nowhere to run from this exposure.[8]

5. Meyers, *Rediscovering Eve*, 72.

6. Rom 16:20; Rev 20:2.

7. Jacobs, *Original Sin*, 90.

8. Brueggemann, *Genesis*, 48.

It is significant that the first element of universal dis-ease concerns the sense of seeing. Adam and Eve had already been naked in the garden but seeing had been safe before—now it is not. Adam and Eve's decision to judge for themselves what is "good" means that innocent seeing has been forever lost. The dis-ease sets in.

## Discuss

- Where do you notice this sense of "dis-ease" at work in human perception today? You might want to consider how this plays out in our use of the internet and social media.

- Do you think it is important to "name" the places of dis-ease through our making, or should we simply show the goodness and beauty that God originally intended?

Throughout the rest of Genesis, sin goes viral, impacting people's relationships with God, with each other, and with creation itself.[9] Adam and Eve's son, Cain, murders his brother. In punishment, the earth that he works as a farmer is cursed (Gen 4:1–8). By the end of chapter 4, Lamach, one of Cain's descendants, boasts triumphantly to his wives that he has murdered a man in retribution for a perceived wrong. Any sensitivity to the shame of sin fast evaporates. Humankind forgets how to blush.

We believe it is important that as makers we explore the *whole* salvation story, and not just the palatable bits. Our making needs to follow the contours of the very real crisis that emerges here, the effects of which are still felt today. The world needs prophetic voices—artists who have the courage and creativity to own the story of original sin as "our story." For some, it will actually be a relief to have the dis-ease named; it may even be their first step into the salvation drama. For example, Peter Hitchens recalls his emotional response to seeing Rogier van der Weyden's painting, *The Last Judgment*:

> Another religious painting. Couldn't these people think of anything else to depict? Still scoffing, I peered at the naked figures fleeing towards the pit of Hell, out of my usual faintly morbid interest in the alleged terrors of damnation. But this time I gasped, my mouth actually hanging open. These people did not appear remote or from the ancient past; they were my own generation.

9. Stackhouse, "Crisis," March 2014.

Because they were naked, they were not imprisoned in their own age by time-bound fashions. . . . They were me, and the people I knew. . . . I had a sudden strong sense of religion being a thing of the present day, not imprisoned under thick layers of time. A large catalogue of misdeeds, ranging from the embarrassing to the appalling, replayed themselves rapidly in my head. I had absolutely no doubt that I was among the damned, if there were any damned. And what if there were? How did I know there were not? I did not know.[10]

Ultimately, this painting played a key role in Hitchen's return to faith.

Read the following extract from a poem by the Jesuit priest, Gerard Manley Hopkins. It registers the *tov*-ness of God's creation, but it also names the effects of sin, particularly on the natural world.

> The world is charged with the grandeur of God.
> It will flame out, like shining from shook foil;
> It gathers to a greatness, like the ooze of oil
> Crushed. Why do men then now not reck his rod?
> Generations have trod, have trod, have trod;
> And all is seared with trade; bleared, smeared with toil;
> And wears man's smudge and shares man's smell: the soil
> Is bare now, nor can foot feel, being shod.

## Reflect

- Where have you seen the world "charged with the grandeur of God"? Take some time to thank God for these things.

- How does this poem bring fresh insight on sin's impact on earth?

- Where do you see "man's smudge" in this world? Start with yourself and your immediate surroundings, then work out to the wider community. Be honest. Name the places of dis-ease and fragmentation in your own life and in your society.

10. Hitchens, as cited in Williams, "Apologetics in 3D."

## The Flood

What happens next is a shocking act of "de-creation" on God's part. In Genesis 6 we gain an insight into God's motives behind it:

> The LORD saw that the wickedness of humankind was great in the earth, and that every inclination of the thoughts of their hearts was only evil continually. And the LORD was sorry that he had made humankind on the earth, and it grieved him to his heart.
> (Gen 6:5–6)

This last sentence is poignant in its simplicity. The sadness that God felt should be remembered as the context for what follows.

Water represented the forces of chaos in much ancient Near-Eastern literature of this period. In creation, God had separated the waters above from the waters below. Now he reverses this act through the flood: all order is swept away and the world returns to chaos. As Greenslade writes: "God's judgment in unleashing the floodwaters represents an undoing of the act of creation. The waters out of which the world was formed—according to Genesis 1—and which were set within bounds, now return unchecked to overwhelm Noah's world in judgment."[11] In your group session you will gain a glimpse into this act of de-creation and the grief behind it.

## Babel: warning to makers

Sin affects every area of human existence, including our vocation as "makers." This next story serves as a warning. Settlers on the plains of Shinar labor to build a great tower—a skyscraper that will reach to the heavens. Instead of working as co-makers with God, they work independently of him, "so that we may make a name for ourselves" (Gen 11:4). This is an audacious act of making.

One of the most famous paintings of the tower of Babel is a Renaissance painting by Pieter Bruegel the Elder.

---

11. Greenslade, *The Big Story*, 68.

**Figure 08:** *The Tower of Babel*
by Pieter Bruegel the Elder, 1563, oil on panel,
Kunsthistorisches Museum, Vienna (114 × 155 cm)

Look at the painting:

- What human activity can you see?
- How much does Bruegel borrow from the Genesis 11 account and how much is contextualized within his own setting of sixteenth-century Antwerp?
- What do you notice about the structure of the tower?
- The frenzied building activity during the Renaissance period led to many art commissions. How might Bruegel's painting be read as a comment on art-making then and serve as a warning to us today?

Rebellion against God leads to fragmentation, particularly of relationships. At Babel, language is confounded and reduced to mere "babble" (Gen 11:7–9). The connection between word and thing, so stable when Adam had named the creatures, begins to break down. This sense of "disconnect" is something that frustrates many writers to this day.

## Covenant promise

After the flood, and despite all that would happen at Babel (and all the other Babels that humankind would build), God makes a covenant with Noah (Gen 9). He promises to uphold the created order and to faithfully continue with his purposes until they reach fulfillment. This they will finally do in Christ. In the next chapter we will meet a man through whom a nation is created, into which nation, one day, God will send his Son. We make, not in order to make a name for ourselves, as they did at Babel, but for the glory of Christ's name.

## Reflect

- What can we learn from the Babel story for our own making?
- How can we allow our art to point to God?
- Write your own covenant with God, humbly putting your creative gifts at his service, for the glory of his name.

## chapter 3

# Calling

Created to live under the blessing of God, Adam and Eve's "calling" was to stay under that blessing. Yet this gift was rejected when they chose to decide what was "good" for themselves.

## Reflect

In the last group session you took part in a de-creative task and reflected on the brokenness that our rebellion brought into the world. What thoughts or images have lingered with you since that task?

God does not give up on his creation, however. Instead, he rolls up his sleeves and, with infinite care and patience, begins creating something even more beautiful and extraordinary than the original design. It's called redemption. This thread runs through the salvation story, finding its fulfillment in Jesus Christ.

After Adam and Eve are banished from the garden, God calls a man—Abram—and from this man he creates a people—Israel—whose vocation it is to live under the blessing of God, in right relationship with him and with each other. This chapter will explore that original calling of Abram's, alongside God's calling on us today, and will consider how our own creative gifts might be used in God's redemption plans.

## Mining our raw material

Just as God gives Adam and Eve raw material and invites them to use it—precious metals to mine, animals to name, a garden to tend—so too with us.[1] We have been born with creative gifts from God. As Michael Novak puts it:

> We didn't give ourselves the personalities, talents, or longings we were born with. When we fulfil these—these gifts from beyond ourselves—it is like fulfilling something we were meant to do. . . . [T]he Creator of all things knows the name of each of us—knows thoroughly, better than we do ourselves, what is in us, for he put it there and intends for us to do something with it—something that meshes with his intentions for many other people. . . . Even if we do not always think of it that way, each of us was given a calling . . . by God.[2]

Jesus tells a parable in which one man was given five talents of money, one two talents, and another one, each according to his ability (Matt 25:14–30). We might feel sympathy for the man who was given only one talent and who did not invest it—the Master's rebuke seems harsh on his return. But a talent was no small sum; in fact, it was worth about twenty years' wages. So too with us. Each of us has been given talents to invest in the kingdom of God, yet some of us are living with buried treasure. It is often in our thirties and forties that these ignored callings start whispering to us.

## Vocation

Another word for "calling" is "vocation," which means so much more than the word "job." "Vocation" is derived from the Latin word *vox,* meaning "voice," and suggests that God is "calling out" those gifts that might be hidden like gold deep within.[3]

This calling could take us into many vocations: it does not have to be a call to Christian ministry. Os Guinness tells the story of William Wilberforce, who nearly missed his calling. After his conversion, Wilberforce was convinced that he should leave politics and enter the ministry; it took a minister to persuade him not to![4] As Ortberg states, your calling may be as varied as:

---

1. See chapter 3 in Ortberg's *If You Want to Walk on Water.*
2. Novak, *Business as a Calling,* 18, 38.
3. It is important to note, as Ortberg points out, that God is the "caller" and you are the "call-ee" here. Ortberg, *If You Want to Walk on Water,* 60.
4. Guinness, *The Call,* 28–29.

the writer resenting a blank screen and hating the deadline, but knowing there is no other joy than that of creating; . . . the gardener who loves to create beauty; the accountant who finds joy in order; the nurse who delights in healing; the mechanic who takes pride in the skill of clever hands.[5]

Responding to God's call has to do with honoring the raw material that God has invested in us.[6] The call is to mine what God has created within us. Each of us is God's "handiwork" or "workmanship," according to Paul, "created in Christ Jesus to do good works, which God prepared in advance for us to do" (Eph 2:10, NIV). The good works Paul has in mind are morally good works, but we might expand on his thought to include aesthetically good works. There is a fully rounded quality to the good for which we are created, and Dewar suggests that God invites us to live "a full-blooded generous living of our giftedness."[7] This next poem by Gerard Manley Hopkins celebrates this full-blooded response.

> As kingfishers catch fire, dragonflies draw flame;
> As tumbled over rim in roundy wells
> Stones ring; like each tucked string tells, each hung bell's
> Bow swung finds tongue to fling out broad its name;
> Each mortal thing does one thing and the same:
> Deals out that being indoors each one dwells;
> Selves—goes itself; *myself* it speaks and spells,
> *Crying What I do is me: for that I came.*[8]

## Reflect

- Read the extract above. How does Hopkins express the uniqueness of each created thing?

- Look at the last two lines in the poem. As you answer the questions below, consider what makes you feel most truly yourself.

---

5. Ortberg, *If You Want to Walk on Water,* 61.

6. Dewar, *Invitations—God's Calling for Everyone,* 3.

7. Ibid.

8. Hopkins, "As Kingfishers Catch Fire."

## 1. What makes you glad?

> Somehow we human beings are never happier than when we are expressing the deepest gifts that are truly us.[9]

> I believe God made me for a purpose, but he also made me fast. And when I run I feel his pleasure.[10]

Some of us tend to divide up our lives between the "sacred" and the "secular." We assume that God is only interested in the former. Francis Dewar recalls his years spent as a vicar, following a call for which he had little heart. He explains his motives: "I had gone into it very much from a sense of duty, impelled by the notion that being a Christian meant doing things you did not want to do: *and that if you liked doing them they probably were not Christian!*"[11]

Listening to what makes us glad, however, is important if we are to persevere for the long haul. Researcher Mihaly Csikszentmihalyi undertook a study with two hundred art school students and interviewed them eighteen years after they had graduated. The results showed that those students who had enrolled in the hope of fame or wealth tended to drift into other professions, while those students who had attended the course because they loved painting for its own sake were nearly all still painting eighteen years later. He concluded:

> Painters must want to paint above all else. If the artist in front of the canvas begins to wonder how much he will sell it for, or what the critics think of it, he won't be able to pursue original avenues. Creative achievement depends on single-minded immersion.[12]

I (Karen) am grateful to my pastor for encouraging me to do this. Years ago, he suggested I take an MA in Christianity and the Arts at King's College, London. At the time, I was juggling motherhood, my job as a teacher, and several commitments at church. Studying felt like an indulgence, much as I loved the sound of the course; moreover, I couldn't see the financial or career benefits of it. However, he suggested I do it just for the love of it. It was a decision I have never once regretted.

---

9. Guinness, *The Call*, 45.
10. Eric Liddell in the film *Chariots of Fire*.
11. Dewar, *Invitations*, 2.
12. Csikszentmihalyi, *Flow*, 157.

Reflect

- Are we prepared to lay our creative longings before God's loving eyes—and to trust him with them? To hold them back may deny him our most treasured possessions.

- When could you say, with Hopkins, "What I do is me: for that I came"? What is it that you love to do? What creative activities have you been drawn to, perhaps since childhood, even if they have been neglected recently?

- Now complete Liddell's statement for yourself:

- When I _____ I feel God's pleasure.


## 2. What makes you sad?

Calling is not just about self-fulfillment, however. The tile fragments from chapter 2 remind us that we walk, daily, through a broken world. Our calling as children of God does not airlift us from this brokenness, but rather brings us into a deeper love for our fractured world, a love that resides at the very heart of God.[13] Beuchner defines calling as "the place where your deep gladness meets the world's deep need."[14]

Kay Warren recalls the day she read a magazine article that woke her up to the plight of the twelve million children who were orphaned in Africa due to HIV/AIDS. Until then she had known no one with AIDS and had felt relatively detached from the issue. Suddenly, as a result of the article, she became sensitized to it. The fate of these children disturbed her. In the following months, it seemed that everywhere she turned, the plight of these children was being talked about. God was calling her. She now heads up an HIV/AIDS initiative at Saddleback Church in Southern California. God can start calling you through what makes you sad.

13. See Rublev's *Icon of the Trinity* in the Introduction.
14. Beuchner, *Wishful Thinking*, 119.

Reflect

What is it in our broken world that most disturbs you? Ask the Holy Spirit to wake you up to what breaks God's heart. You might want to use Samuel's words as a prayer: "Speak, Lord, for your servant is listening" (1 Sam 3:9).

_____

_____

## 3. What makes you mad?

Anger has long been identified as a great driving force, not least for the prophet-poets of the Bible. Moses had anger issues, but God was often able to harness this anger for his purposes.

In the poetry collection *Learning to Love,* poet and social-care manager Chris Goan recalls his anger when welfare benefits were cut and he witnessed the impact on the poor. His anger acted as a catalyst in adopting a new creative medium: protest poetry. He writes:

> The frustration and impotence I felt in the face of this became something I started to write about as a means of protest.
>
> It occurred to me that this is what poetry was for. Poetry should be prophetic—not in the sense of telling our fortune, but more by telling us something of what we are—warts and all. . . . It should be an honest, engaged, hopeful critique of culture. . . . It should be a mirror lit by harsh light revealing the powerful in their undressed state. . . .
>
> If we have a voice, we should use it—not just for saying pretty things, . . . but also in saying hard things, difficult things, because art with nothing to say is simply wallpaper.[15]

Anger at injustice can be channeled into truth-telling. Doing this creatively can engage people's imaginations in a way that a direct rant may not, as any good satirist knows.

The novel *Uncle Tom's Cabin* exposed the blight of slavery on America's moral landscape, but did so in a way that political tracts and speeches failed to do. The author, Harriet Beecher-Stowe, succeeded in doing what Emily Dickinson advised: "Tell all the truth but tell it slant."[16] Her story stirred a

15. Goan, "Protest Poetry," *Learning to Love,* 98–99.
16. Dickinson, *The Collected Poems of Emily Dickinson.*

nation's dis-ease about slavery, and many feel that this culminated in the Civil War. In fact, legend has it that when Abraham Lincoln met Beecher-Stowe in 1862, he greeted her with the words, "So this is the little woman who wrote the book that started this great war!"[17]

## Reflect

What makes you red-hot mad? Where has God revealed to you an injustice in his world that needs a creative voicing?

---

---

## Abram's Call

It should be apparent by now that what we are talking about here is not an individualist's "follow your dreams" idea of calling. Nor is it about "finding yourself." In fact, the individual we will now meet has to *lose himself* in one sense in order to follow God's call. Ultimately, the calling is a call into God's story. Take God's calling of the people of Israel. What if, asks Abraham Heschel, Israel exists in order to dream the dreams of God?[18] Our highest calling, as we will see in the chapter 10, is surely to dwell inside God's own imagination and to live out *his* dreams of redemption for this world.

"Call" (*qara'*) has a straightforward meaning in Old Testament Hebrew that is similar to ours. When you "call" someone you get their attention, you catch their ear.[19] Abram is not young when God catches his ear.[20] From a settled existence in the sophisticated society of Babylonia, this seventy-five-year-old man leaves his native country and takes on the life of a nomad, trekking across the desert through unfamiliar territory to the land of Canaan.[21]

---

17. Yancey, *Vanishing Grace*, 118.
18. Heschel, *Moral Grandeur and Spiritual Audacity*, 237.
19. Guinness, *The Call*, 29.
20. The story of Abram's call can be read in Genesis 12:1–9.
21. Greenslade, *The Big Story*, 148.

There seems to be nothing remarkable about Abram when we first meet him. No reason is given for God's calling *him* as opposed to anyone else and, as his story unfolds, he hardly emerges a flawless hero. God is the real hero in this story, promising to be pro-active in giving Abram land (Gen 12:1, 7), descendants (Gen 12:2), and blessing (Gen 12:2–3). Abram is called into the salvation story at *God's* initiative, as are we.

## Seeds of promise

However, it is important to take hold of a call. Abram holds onto God's promise in faith. For twenty-five years, Abram sees no sign of a son. How can he birth a people when he cannot even conceive *one child*? It must have seemed absurd. Holding onto God's promise is sometimes far more difficult than taking hold of it in the first place.

In his book *The Journey of Desire*, John Eldredge tells the story of a sea lion that has lost the sea. He finds himself in a dry and dusty desert with only a mud puddle in which to bathe. At night, he climbs onto a rock to catch the sea breeze—and the distant scent stirs dreams of home. However, eventually he finds excuses to stop visiting the rock: "I have too much to do," he says. "I cannot waste my time idling about." Yet, writes Eldredge, he did not really have too much to do. "The truth of it was, waking so far from home was such a disappointment, he did not want to have those wonderful dreams anymore."[22]

Holding onto the promises of God is not easy for Abram, and on more than one occasion he makes do with a mud puddle.[23] Sometimes it is hard to face our desire for the sea. The dusty desert is a comforting known. "What if I can't make it?" "What if it's just a mirage?" The temptation is to persuade ourselves that this is as good as it gets. Yet one night, in his mercy, God lifts Abram's head to the skies in reassurance.

## Read

> After these things the word of the LORD came unto Abram in a vision, saying, Fear not, Abram: I am thy shield, and thy exceeding great reward.

22. Eldredge, *The Journey of Desire*, 50.

23. First seeking to leave an inheritance through Eliezer, his servant, then sleeping with Hagar, Sara's maidservant, in order to produce a son.

And Abram said, LORD God, what wilt thou give me, seeing I go childless, and the steward of my house is this Eliezer of Damascus?

And Abram said, Behold, to me thou hast given no seed: and, lo, one born in my house is mine heir.

And, behold, the word of the LORD came unto him, saying, This shall not be thine heir; but he that shall come forth out of thine own bowels shall be thine heir.

And he brought him forth abroad, and said, Look now toward heaven, and tell the stars, if thou be able to number them: and he said unto him, So shall thy seed be.

And he believed in the LORD; and he counted it to him for righteousness. (Gen 15:1–6, KJV)

## Respond

The painting below explores God's promise. Spend some time looking at it. What do you see here?

**Figure 09:** *Promise*
**by Gill C. Sakakini, 2007, textile (4' x 5')**

- Why do you think God asks Abram to look up at the stars in the night sky?
- What effect do the dandelion seeds in this image have in representing the stars? What potential is suggested in them?
- Think about the journey of these seeds. How much control does one have over their journey and final destination?

Look back on your own faith journey and consider the seeds of promise that God has sown in you. Jot down some ideas for the following:

1. Gifts that are currently being cultivated/nurtured in me:

_____

2. Gifts lying dormant:

_____

These are gifts that seem to have fallen asleep. What would help you to develop these gifts again? Circle as appropriate: time/motivation/courage/opportunity to use them.

3. Gifts I don't have:

_____

Ortberg points out that honoring a raw material means knowing the potential of the material: what it can do and what it can't. "Skilled potters know that as they knead and press clay, it presses back, telling them what it can and cannot become."[24] I (Karen) was once asked to consider working for an organization to reach out to the local community through hospitality. It was a vision that really chimed with my heart for outreach. However, when I told my husband about it later, he fell about laughing. The job involved a lot of cooking. And while I cook, he reminded me, it's not something that makes me particularly glad. In fact, whenever we entertain, he's the one

24. Ortberg, *If You Want to Walk on Water*, 60. Ortberg warns us to beware of the subculture that promises that you can do anything you want to, be anything you want to be, if you make the effort. He quotes Parker Palmer: "The message was that both the universe and I were without limits, given enough energy and commitment on my part. God made things that way, and all I had to do was to get with the program. My troubles began, of course, when I started to slam into my limitations, especially in the form of failure." Parker, *Let Your Life Speak*, 66.

who likes cooking and I'm happier chatting to people. I'm also one of those mothers who buys cakes for the school fair and then cheats by icing them at home. So I said no. Discerning your potential involves discerning your limits as well as your strengths.

What do you think are the limits of your raw material? You might want to ask someone else to help identify these with you!

4. Gifts that have come to fruition:

_____

Where do you see your gifts reaching fulfillment and being used to bless others? Find a way to celebrate these gifts with someone who wants you to flourish!

## Abram believed

What Abram does next is pivotal. "Abram *believed* the LORD, and the LORD counted him as righteous because of his faith" (Gen 15:6). Abram *chose to hold onto the promise—in faith*. However, faith doesn't stop him from asking for reassurance. After being shown this sign in the night sky, Abram asks, "how can I know?" (Gen 15:8). Rather than blasting Abram off the face of the earth, God makes a covenant with him (Gen 15:7–21)—a "binding agreement," the kind made in marriage. Traditionally in a covenant, both parties make promises to be faithful to each other. Animals are slain, the meat is walked around in a figure of eight, and threats are issued if the covenant is broken. However, in this covenant, Abram is sound asleep! Yet again, it is all undeserved, absurdly generous *gift from God*. Perhaps it's hardly surprising that when the promised child, Isaac, is finally born he is given a name that means, "he will laugh."[25]

25. Altar, *The Five Books of Moses*, 322.

## Who am I?

The promise to make Abram into a people of God begins to be realized much later, in the exodus. Abraham's descendants are called out of slavery to worship God: that is to be their ultimate vocation, as it is ours (Exod 7:16; 8:1; 9:1). Through Moses, God gives the people an identity and forms them into a community.

Moses feels inadequate for the job: "Who am I?" he asks. It's a good point. An exile from Egypt, an outlaw, and a mere shepherd,[26] Moses is hardly promising material for this challenge. Significantly, God doesn't "recruit" Moses by telling him how well suited Moses is for the job. As Max Lucado states, persuasive points might have included: "Who better understands the culture than a former prince?" or "How well equipped he will be for wilderness travel," but these are points God fails to make.[27] Instead, when Moses asks, "Who am I?" God simply replies, "For I will be with you." Hardly an answer at all. So Moses fires a second question: "And who are you?" And God answers in a seeming riddle: YHWH.

In calling Moses, it is significant that God reveals *himself*. The name "YHWH" spans tense and time and means something like "I am who I am" and "I will be who I will be." It also has connotations of longevity, meaning something like "I Am He Who Endures."[28] What matters most is not who or what Moses is, but *who and what God is—and that he will be with Moses*. Ultimately, this is what matters most in our calling too. It is God's voice that does the calling and it is his name that underwrites that call.

## Make

Draw, write, engrave, embroider, or paint the divine name—whether in English as YHWH, or in Hebrew as יהוה—creating large letters. As you move your hand across what you are making, ask God to reveal more of himself as he calls you. Pray that he would underwrite your vocation. Take what you make along to your group session.

---

26. Ibid., 320.
27. Lucado, *The Great House of God*, 27.
28. Ibid.

## Watch out for stumbling blocks

There are many things that can act as stumbling blocks as we seek to respond to God's call. We may be paralysed by perfectionism and fear. We cannot bear to make a mistake, so we take no steps at all. Another common obstacle is that of comparison. Francis Dewar tells the story of Rabbi Zuscha who, on his deathbed, was asked what he thought life held beyond the grave. He thought for a while and then responded: "I don't really know. But one thing I do know: when I get there I am not going to be asked, 'Why weren't you Moses?' Or 'Why weren't you David?' I am going to be asked, 'Why weren't you Zuscha?'"[29]

Some of us are avid surfers of gocompare.com. We are so busy thinking about everyone else's calling that the voice of the Caller gets drowned out for us. Peter stumbles into this obstacle at the beach. Jesus is re-commissioning him to pastoral ministry, but Peter gets distracted by the disciple whom Jesus loved and asks, "Lord, what about him?" to which Jesus swiftly responds, "None of your business!"[30] Peter just needs to do what *he* is called to do and not to worry about everyone else's calling.

Moses also falls into the trap of comparison. As Ortberg writes:

> God called Moses: "Go to Pharaoh—the most powerful man on earth. Tell him to let his labor force leave without compensation to worship a god he doesn't believe in. Then convince a timid, stiff-necked people to run away into the desert. That's your calling. "And Moses said: Here am I. Send Aaron."[31]

Comparison can stunt the development of a calling. Years ago I (Karen) led a team of women, all of whom had different gifts. I remember one particular team member who had a beautiful singing voice. Others would often complain, "I'm not gifted like her!" to which I would want to retort, "No, you're gifted like YOU!" They each had amazing gifts—creative ways of showing God's hospitality; a huge capacity to love the smallest and the least amongst us. There are many ways the world needs to hear God's song.

Comparison not only cripples us, it can cripple others. When the singer becomes aware of others' envy, she may be afraid to raise her voice. Elizabeth O'Connor reflects on this with Herod:

29. Dewar, *Invitations—God's Calling for Everyone*, 15.

30. My paraphrase. See John 21:15–23.

31. Ortberg, *If You Want to Walk on Water*, 69.

Thought today of envy—the envy of Herod. It is a dread thought that another should take my place—another be considered greater than I. Kill off the possibility of replacement. . . . As for the exercising of gifts, let everyone be cautious. The exercising of gifts evokes envy—makes enemies of those who, if you stay commonplace—would be your friends. Above all, do not exercise the gift of being yourself—this is the greatest threat of all.[32]

How many people's callings have been crippled by such threats? Yet our Creator has gifted us with unique raw material that he wants us to invest in his kingdom. So let's stop surfing gocompare.com and listen out for his voice across all the noise!

## Sleeping beauty

Others may not be paralyzed by comparison so much as lulled to sleep. Disconnected from the outside world, they feel immune to it. The reasons for such slumber are many, but to those people, we believe God comes and says, "*Wake up, sleeper*" (Eph 5:14).[33] Roll up your sleeves and take part in the dreams of our Creator-Redeemer God in this broken world.

This next poem by Charlotte Mew explores just such an awakening:

### The Call

From our low seat beside the fire
Where we have dozed and dreamed and watched the glow
Or raked the ashes, stopping so
We scarcely saw the sun or rain
Above, or looked much higher
Than this same quiet red or burned-out fire.
Tonight we heard a call,
A rattle on the window pane,
A voice on the sharp air,
And felt a breath stirring our hair,
A flame within us:
Something swift and tall
Swept in and out and that was all.

---

32. O'Connor, *Eighth Day of Creation,* as cited in Dewar, *Invitations,* 100.

33. See also O'Connor, *Cry Pain, Cry Hope,* as cited in Dewar, *Invitations,* 13.

Was it a bright or a dark angel?
Who can know?
It left no mark upon the snow,
But suddenly it snapped the chain
Unbarred, flung wide the door
Which will not shut again;
And so we cannot sit here any more.
We must arise and go:
The world is cold without
And dark and hedged about
With mystery and enmity and doubt,
But we must go
Though yet we do not know
Who called, or what marks we shall leave upon the snow.[34]

## Reflect

- In what way does the speaker seem to be asleep at the start of this poem?
- How does the narrator perceive the call?
- What sense of compulsion is felt in response?
- Is there anything in this poem that resonates with or disrupts your own experience of hearing God calling you?

Charlotte Mews describes a door that "will not shut again." As O'Connor states, "People alive to God's calling are not the same people at the end of their story that they were in the beginning."[35] Abram was renamed Abraham; Jacob Israel. One thing is certain: when you respond to God's call, prepare to be changed.

---

34. Mew, "The Call," in Morley, *The Heart's Time*, 25.
35. O'Connor, *Cry Pain, Cry Hope*, as cited in Dewar, *Invitations*, 15.

## chapter 4

# Conception

## The Annunciation

Over the centuries, artists have attempted to capture the moment in history when God broke into our time and space, sending his Son in human form. The act of conception was preceded by a word from God, and the declaration of this good news has come to be called "the annunciation." The event is recorded in Luke's Gospel in a dialogue between the archangel Gabriel and a humble girl called Mary—who chose to say "Yes" to God.

### Read

Read the passage below, slowly.

> In the sixth month the angel Gabriel was sent by God to a town in Galilee called Nazareth, to a virgin engaged to a man whose name was Joseph, of the house of David. The virgin's name was Mary. And he came to her and said, "Greetings, favored one! The Lord is with you." But she was much perplexed by his words and pondered what sort of greeting this might be. The angel said to her, "Do not be afraid, Mary, for you have found favor with God. And now, you will conceive in your womb and bear a son, and you will name him Jesus. He will be great and will be called the Son of the Most High, and the Lord God will give to him the throne of his ancestor David. He will reign over the house of Jacob for ever, and of his kingdom there will be no end." Mary said to the angel,

"How can this be, since I am a virgin?" The angel said to her, "The Holy Spirit will come upon you, and the power of the Most High will overshadow you; therefore the child to be born will be holy; he will be called Son of God. And now, your relative Elizabeth in her old age has also conceived a son; and this is the sixth month for her who was said to be barren. For nothing will be impossible with God." Then Mary said, "Here am I, the servant of the Lord; let it be with me according to your word." Then the angel departed from her. (Luke 1:26–38)

## Respond

The annunciation was a popular theme for artists, particularly in the early Renaissance. Fra Roberto Caracciolo da Lecce, a famous fifteenth-century Italian preacher, identified five spiritual and mental states attributable to Mary, and over the years different artists have sought to capture them. These states are:

- *conturbatio* (disquiet/"troubled")
- *cogitatio* (reflection)
- *interrogatio* (inquiry—"How this shall be?")
- *humilitatio* (submission)
- *meritatio* (merit—this is the moment when Christ, God incarnate, enters Mary's womb)[1]

1. Read through the passage in Luke again. Can you find examples of the states outlined above?

2. Now look at the painting beneath by Fra Filippo Lippi. Which "state" does Lippi capture in the painting?

---

1. Baxandall, *Painting and Experience in Fifteenth Century Italy*, 55–56.

Figure 10: *The Annunciation*
by Fra Filippo Lippi, c. 1450–53,
The National Gallery, London (68.6 cm x 152.7 cm)

## Lippi's *Annunciation*

Lippe's panel is believed to have hung in a principal bedchamber in the Medici palace in Florence, one that was probably used as a bridal chamber. This context deepens the intimacy of the painting and the idea of God's conceptions in our lives through Christ. In the scene we are drawn into a moment of deep encounter. Framed within the lunette-shaped painting, the archangel, seen on bended knee, leans in towards Mary. In return, Mary leans in to what God is doing before her very eyes. The encounter in Luke's Gospel has engaged the imagination of many artists and poets as a beautifully caught, timeless moment. Edwin Muir seeks to capture this here:

> But through the endless afternoon
> These neither speak nor movement make,
> But stare into their deepening trance
> As if their gaze would never break.[2]

In many ways Lippi's panel follows conventional iconography for an annunciation painting. Conventionally, Mary reads from Scripture, and the rays spray out over the book, linking this splash of light to the Word of God. The panel divides into three spaces and the narrative reads along the horizontal axis, from left to right. The architecture surrounding Mary

2. Muir, "The Annunciation."

suggests both "enclosure and openness"; Mary is both secluded from the world and yet available to God.[3] The distance created between her and Gabriel provides a central space for God's intervention; the horizontal axis is interrupted by the vertical, where the hand of God appears in a cloud, perhaps symbolizing Mary's "overshadowing" by "the power of the Most High." We are reminded that without God's intervention this conception would not have happened. Borrowing from the accounts of Jesus' baptism, the Holy Spirit is represented by a dove and our eyes are invited to follow its spiraling journey, from God's hand above to the woman below.

Unlike Duccio's *Annunciation* or Lippi's San Lorenzo *Annunciations*, which depict Mary as "troubled," some believe that Lippi captures her at the point of humble submission. The greeting, the exclamation, the questions—all are now exhausted; Mary finally gives her consent with the words: "Behold the handmaid of the Lord; be it unto me according to thy word" (Luke 1:38). In humility, she leans forward to receive. The art historian Leo Steinberg believes that Lippi is painting in response to Mary's earlier state when she asked, "How shall this be?" He interprets her question less as an incredulous one (i.e., "How shall this be? It's impossible!"), and more as a practical one (i.e., "How shall this be—by what means?").[4] And in answering the "How?" Lippi uses the language of vision.

*An open eye*

If you look closely at the dove's descent,[5] you will notice some faint gold spirals, almost faded now, which follow in the dove's wake, sent from God's hand above. The image of light is often used to signify God's Word, finally embodied by Jesus Christ, according to John's Gospel. Renaissance artists picked up this theme and, conventionally, Lippi's dove emits rays of light from its beak—the Word springs forth. Less conventionally, however, Lippi depicts a burst of light coming from the slit in Mary's tunic by her stomach. This light represents her own response.

3. Drury, *Painting the Word*, 48.

4. Steinberg, *"How Shall This Be?,"* 25.

5. This can be viewed on the National Gallery, London's website (https://www. nationalgallery.org.uk/paintings/fra-filippo-lippi-the-annunciation). Zoom in on the detail around Mary's stomach.

**Figure 11: Detail of *The Annunciation***
by Fra Filippo Lippi, c. 1450–53,
The National Gallery, London (68.6 cm x 152.7 cm)

The Latin and Italian word *tunica* had two meanings in the 1400s: the first referred to a long dress, the second to the layered membranes that surround and protect the eye.[6] This protective "tunic" would part at what was called *il foro*, "the opening or doorway" to the eye. So what we are seeing in the slit of Mary's dress is essentially an open eye. In Lippi's painting, Christ, the living Word, *bursts in on Mary*; she, in turn, *jumps forward to welcome him in*—and in this moment we have conception.

So Mary has an open eye. Yet the painting's architecture reminds us that Mary's eye is also enclosed. A strong relationship exists between "purity" and "seeing" in this painting. Unlike Eve's seeing in Genesis 3, Mary's seeing is protected. The conventional symbolism of Lippi's architectural

6. Drury, *Painting the Word*, 53.

43

space suggests that boundaries exist for her. She is the *hortus conclusus,* the enclosed garden, a notion borrowed from the Song of Songs (4:12) and developed by the patristic writers. Motifs like the lily, common in annunciation paintings, reinforce this.

Matthew's Gospel alludes to this relationship between purity and seeing. In the Beatitudes, Jesus states: "Blessed are the pure in heart, for they will see God" (Matt 5:8), and Matthew later records Jesus saying: "The light of the body is the eye: if therefore thine eye be single thy whole body shall be full of light" (Matt 6:22). Mary seems to have an "eye of light" in this painting.[7] In Luke's Gospel, she is hailed as "highly favored" by God (Luke 1:28), represented here by the sign of the blessing, extending from both the hand of Gabriel and of God. Perhaps Mary embodies Jesus' promise: "For whoever has, to him more shall be given, and he will have an abundance" (Matt 13:12).

*Saying "Yes"*

Lippi's *Annunciation* seems to capture a suspended moment in time; a caught breath. Could it be that this relates as much to what is happening in the heavens as it does on earth? Perhaps God was waiting for Mary to say "Yes," for he will not force himself on anyone. Drury suggests that Lippi's painting reminds us that God is just waiting for "that little moving-forward in consent."[8]

This theme of consent is explored in this next poem by Denise Levertov:

**Annunciation**
We know the scene: the room, variously furnished,
almost always a lectern, a book; always
the tall lily.
    Arrived on solemn grandeur of great wings,
the angelic ambassador, standing or hovering,
whom she acknowledges, a guest.
But we are told of meek obedience. No one mentions
courage.

7. Pickstock, "What Shines Between," 120. Pickstock explores the idea of Mary's "careful gaze" in this chapter.

8. Drury, *Painting the Word,* 53.

The engendering Spirit
did not enter her without consent.
    God waited.
She was free
to accept or to refuse, choice
integral to humanness.

———————————————

Aren't there annunciations
of one sort or another
in most lives?
    Some unwillingly
undertake great destinies,
enact them in sullen pride,
uncomprehending.
More often
those moments
    when roads of light and storm
    open from darkness in a man or woman,
are turned away from
in dread, in a wave of weakness, in despair
and with relief.
Ordinary lives continue.
                God does not smite them.
But the gates close, the pathway vanishes . . . .

. . . This was the moment no one speaks of,
when she could still refuse.

A breath unbreathed,
             Spirit,

                    suspended,

                        waiting.

———————————————

She did not cry, "I cannot. I am not worthy,"
Nor, "I have not the strength."
She did not submit with gritted teeth,

raging, coerced.

Bravest of all humans,
consent illumined her.
The room filled with its light,
the lily glowed in it,
and the iridescent wings.
Consent,
courage unparalleled,
opened her utterly.[9]

## Reflect

What good news has God "announced" to you? Here are some ideas to get you started:

- That you are unique to him, precious enough to send his Son, Jesus Christ, to draw you into relationship with the Father, Son, and Spirit.
- That you are called into God's redeeming purposes for this world and that you have a part to play in his story.
- That he has given you creative gifts that bring him delight.
- Now you continue! Get particular. Think about "announcements" that God has made to you.

## Finding an Elizabeth

### Nurture in the dark

It takes courage to say "Yes" to God. In Mary's case, she was "opened . . . utterly," as Levertov states, not only to the gift of Christ's birth, but also to his death. Any conception of his will take a cruciform shape in our lives. Not only will it take courage to say "Yes" to God's announcements, it will also take courage to carry those conceptions to term.

A conception is nurtured in the darkness and protection of the womb, and Mary seems to be discerning about sharing the news. Just as a seed needs to be underground, so an embryo needs to grow in the dark of a

9. Levertov, "Annunciation," from *A Door in the Hive* in *New Selected Poems*. Reproduced with permission of Bloodaxe Books.

mother's womb. Bring it to light too soon and it could be stillborn. Later, as Jesus grows, Luke records that Mary "treasured" these things in her heart concerning him (Luke 2:19, 51). There is a place of internal pondering and treasuring in Mary, and in this we would be wise to learn.

The writer Marilynne Robinson records hiding poems under her bed as a child, not because she had anything against her family or any potential reader, but simply because, "there's something about me that wants to be secretive until I feel that something is done."[10] In our own creative growth, when God brings something to gestation, it needs protection in order to take shape. Rilke expresses this in *Letters to a Young Poet*:

> *Everything* is gestation and then bringing forth. To let each impression and each germ of a feeling come to completion wholly in itself, in the dark, in the inexpressible, the unconscious, beyond the reach of one's own intelligence, and await with deep humility and patience the birth-hour of a new clarity.[11]

Alan Bennett likens the place where creative projects grow to "a photographic darkroom where images are developed, where things are brought to light."[12] This is something that a nest can provide, as explored in the poem below.

**Nest in Winter**
With each tireless gust
the hedge is stripped of froth
and pared to Japanese print.
Yet hid in winter's loss
last year's cradles are exposed
to looking eyes
that scan the lane
and stop at a haiku of twigs.

A densely woven order, lined
with moss and wool and down;
a home once veiled
from hungry eyes, now exposed

10. Robinson, "The Deeper Mind," Interview in *Poets and Writers*.

11. Rilke, *Letters to a Young Poet*, as cited in Dewar, *Invitations*, 25.

12. Alan Bennett, as cited in Dewer, *Invitations*, 25.

in winter's skeletal quiet.

Here is a place that hid some life
fragile and translucent,
where wings worked form, grew curious
and then rehearsed for flight.
Perhaps we need these hidden nests
to nurture our conceptions?
For "Mary treasured up these things"
and did her thinking in the dark.[13]

## Bringing it to light

Mary might be cautious about sharing news of this conception, but she does nonetheless share it with someone. Gabriel informs Mary that her aged relative Elizabeth has also conceived a son (Luke 1:36) and Mary subsequently sets out with haste to visit her (Luke 1:39). This would have probably involved a ten-day journey.

While Luke is silent about Mary's motives, it is clear that Elizabeth is a sign of the promise. The pregnancy of her cousin at such an old age must be assurance to Mary that the Lord is indeed God of her conception. Just as John the Baptist will become something of a "forerunner" to Jesus, so Elizabeth becomes a forerunner to Mary. When they greet each other, Elizabeth's child confirms whom Mary is carrying: ". . . as soon as I heard the sound of your greeting, the child in my womb leapt for joy" (Luke 1:44). Elizabeth then blesses Mary for holding the promise: "And blessed is she who believed that there would be a fulfillment of what was spoken to her by the Lord" (Luke 1:45). This is not just a story about "me and God"; we find our voices in a community of faith. Mary is intentional about finding Elizabeth as she holds the promise in faith. As Heidi Baker states:

> When God places a promise inside us, we have to decide to nurture it and believe that it will be accomplished. Every word God has ever given me required me to be patient and tenacious in walking it out. I have had to make choices and decisions that align with His promises. Saying yes to Him is not something I can do

---

13. Case-Green, "Nest in Winter."

once and then forget about it. I have to live out that yes every day of my life.[14]

Mary stays with Elizabeth for about the first three months, which is often the most vulnerable period in a pregnancy. Together, they hold the promise with prophetic hope.

## Reflect

- "Mary stored up all these things . . . ." How easy do you find it to nurture a conception in the dark? How might you create a "photographic darkroom" or "nest" in which your own creativity can develop?

- Why was it so important for Mary to find an Elizabeth? You might like to consider some of the things in the footnote below.[15]

- Do you have an "Elizabeth" in your life? Would you like to pray for one?

## Labor

It is important to have conceptions confirmed and celebrated mid-way by an Elizabeth because one thing is sure: from conception to labor, there will be hard graft involved! This is something that artist Paul Soupiset discovered when he labored to bring to birth a labyrinth project in San Antonio, Texas. He recorded the project's progress on a Lenten blog in 2008[16] in which we see the many heavy stones that had to be moved, along with the occasional scorpion!

---

14. Baker, *Birthing the Miraculous*, 109.

15. Points might include: the danger of false pregnancies; doubt ("Did I really hear?" "Did God really say?" Watch out for the word-twister in chapter 2!); a need for encouragement as she carries the conception to term.

16. You can find details at soupiest.typepad.com.

**Figure 12:** *Forming the Switchbacks*
**by the Labyrinth Project, April 16, 2008, San Antonio**[17]

Paul Soupiset's poem below captures the graft involved.

the hour growing late,
pregnant
with this project, with possibilities,
i lifted the front edge of my
tee-shirt to form a chalky cloth sling

i piled in hands full of
fist-sized limestone
three, nine, thirty-eight,
and i labored to stand,
grabbing my back,
looking and feeling
like a last-trimester mama—
and i laughed out loud
this father of four births,
four umbilical incisions,
four afterbirths,

17. Courtesy of Paul Soupiset.

and one miscarriage,
waddling over to this
birthing site,
pacing in artistic anticipation,
wondering and worrying
about this strange,
forthcoming delivery . . .

so many strong women
in my life,
many of them mothers,
and some of them
wing-waiting

i figured they'd all
laugh out loud
(perhaps my twin-bearing
mom the loudest)
to see me wrestle and
wrangle and huff

i came around
to where i'd left off

i couldn't gracefully
set my quarry upon the earth
so i squatted
and, valsalva,
let the stones

fall

a little lower than the angels
had the earth tonight been water
the concentric rippled labyrinth
might have serv'd witness enough

to the father son and holy ghost.[18]

Soupiset's blog reveals the loneliness that this creative work can involve, and the need for community. There will indeed be "wrestle and wrangle and huff" involved. Yet we look forward to the joy of the birth.

## The Magnificat

It is no surprise, therefore that after confirming what God has conceived in Mary, Elizabeth helps her to celebrate. Upon meeting Elizabeth, Mary seems to find her voice: her response to God's action is a glorifying, creative burst, and her song has come to be known as the Magnificat (Luke 1:46–55). It begins with those memorable words:

> My soul magnifies the Lord,
> and my spirit rejoices in God my Savior . . .

The song is soaked in Scripture: quotation after quotation come pouring out, much of it taken from Hannah's own song in 1 Samuel 2. Mary voices these texts afresh. Note that all the glory is reflected back to God; none is absorbed by Mary.

Yet the Magnificat also reminds us of a battle being waged. Rather than being a sweet, fluffy baby-shower offering, the imagery is militaristic and combative. Mary reminds us that God's kingdom means God's justice:

> He has shown strength with his arm;
> he has scattered the proud in the thoughts of their hearts.
> He has brought down the powerful from their thrones,
> and lifted up the lowly;
> (Luke 1:51–52)

Note that these words are declared *before* Jesus has even been born. Mary is voicing a prophetic hope. In the words of Tom Wright: "It's the gospel before the gospel, a fierce bright shout of triumph thirty weeks before Bethlehem, thirty years before Calvary and Easter. It goes with swing and a clap and a stamp. It's all about God, and it's all about revolution."[19]

It is good to celebrate with a creative "Yes" what we want to see more of: God's kingdom on earth as it is in heaven; God's justice turning this

18. Soupiset, "The Labyrinth Project," Lentenblog.
19. Wright, *Luke for Everyone*, 14.

world's power structures upside down. We need Magnificat-makers. Don't be shy about this. This is not about honouring ourselves; it is about honouring and affirming what *God has done* and *is doing*—in us and for us. May what we make artistically help to cultivate a culture of celebration of God's hand at work.

## Make

Take one aspect of this conception story in Luke's Gospel and imagine yourself responding to it. You could choose from the following:

- Gabriel's visit to Mary
- Mary's response to the startling news
- The idea of nurturing/treasuring a conception in safety
- Finding an Elizabeth. (You could adopt Elizabeth's perspective or Mary's here)
- The Magnificat
- Labor

Let your imagination roam this part of the story. Choose a medium, visual or verbal, and start making something in response. Bring what you have started making, along with any materials you need, to the group session.

## The Project

Mary found her voice—and the Magnificat was the creative result. How are you finding your voice creatively? Over the next few weeks we invite you to image something of God's story and to contribute this piece to a group project. It could be through the creative media of painting, writing (poetry or prose), textiles, ceramics, woodwork, mixed media art, photography, weaving, sculpture, printing, or other.[20] Alternatively, you could contribute something you have made in one of the "Make" tasks in this book.

The project is outlined in more detail in Appendix 2.

---

20. Dance or movement and music are also possible—just check with your group leader that there will be space to perform. If not, you could try filming it.

## chapter 5

# Coming

## Christ at the core

Here we arrive at the crux of the story, the pivotal moment in which the main character, Jesus the Word, present at creation with the Father and the Holy Spirit (John 1:1–2), becomes flesh and makes an unobtrusive entrance with dramatic consequences—right on cue. The apostle John's eagle, described in chapter 1 closes in on the event of Jesus' incarnation and hovers at the threshold between the old order and the new (John 1:17–18). This is a thin place, described in Celtic Christianity as an in-between moment where we see the intersection of two worlds through something like a veil. The words of Old Testament prophets point to the coming of Christ in a variety of ways, for example, Isaiah declares: "Therefore the LORD himself will give you a sign. Look, the young woman is with child and shall bear a son, and shall name him Immanuel" (Isa 7:14). Hosea showed God's generous heart for his recalcitrant people by saying, "When Israel was a child, I loved him, and out of Egypt I called my son" (Hos 11:1). In Psalm 2 the liminal moment is characterized by a collision of two orders—the conspiring nations and kings of the earth are called to account (Ps 2:1–2) in light of the coming Messiah. This psalm speaks up and says more than we know about the present reality of warring and plotting by pointing forward to the fulfillment of God's plan with a caution to be wise in view of God's coming to earth in human form. In Proverbs 8:22–31 wisdom is personified as creatively present with the Trinity at the beginning, before Jesus would become incarnate.

> The LORD possessed me in the beginning of his ways, before he made any thing from the beginning.
>
> I was set up from eternity, and of old before the earth was made.
>
> The depths were not as yet, and I was already conceived; neither had the fountains of waters as yet sprung out:
>
> The mountains with their huge bulk had not as yet been established: before the hills I was brought forth:
>
> He had not yet made the earth, nor the rivers, nor the poles of the world.
>
> When he prepared the heavens, I was present: when with a certain law and compass he enclosed the depths:
>
> When he established the sky above, and poised the fountains of waters:
>
> When he compassed the sea with its bounds, and set a law to the waters that they should not pass their limits: when be balanced the foundations of the earth;
>
> I was with him forming all things: and was delighted every day, playing before him at all times;
>
> Playing in the world: and my delights were to be with the children of men. (Prov 8:22-31)[1]

From a much later vantage point, but in equally beautiful prose (which may be borrowed), Paul writes "The Hymn to Christ" (Col 1:15–20). He is at pains to communicate to the Colossians the utter supremacy of Christ in the face of a heresy that implied that something additional to Jesus was required for salvation. He emphasizes that Christ is central to *everything*.

## Read

> He is the image of the invisible God, the firstborn of all creation; for in him all things in heaven and on earth were created, things visible and invisible, whether thrones or dominions or rulers or powers—all things have been created through him and for him. He himself is before all things, and in him all things hold together. He is the head of the body, the church; he is the beginning, the firstborn from the dead, so that he might come to have first place

---

1. Douay-Rheims 1899 American Edition Version.

in everything. For in him all the fullness of God was pleased to dwell, and through him God was pleased to reconcile to himself all things, whether on earth or in heaven, by making peace through the blood of his cross. (Col 1:15–20)

## Respond

- Fold a piece of paper or a sketchbook page in half then open it out flat.
- On one half, using acrylic or quick-drying paint in one or more colors, create an abstract design in a loose strokes.
- Fold the paper over to make a print on the other side by pressing firmly but carefully.
- Unfold the paper and allow to dry. Reflect for a few moments: how does Jesus show us what God is like. How does this affect your view of yourself as an image-bearer?
- Cut or tear three sorts of paper into pieces of any size and shape. Make three stacks. The following are suitable: newspaper, colored paper, tissue paper, lightly patterned scraps.
- Read the text and write words that describe Jesus on paper from the first stack (e.g., "image"). You can handwrite or use cut-out or ink-stamp letters.
- Read again and write verbs (action words) on the second stack (e.g., "created").
- Re-read, and on the final stack write the subject of the sentences (i.e., the person who is performing the action).
- Consider these words. Note repetitions, similarities, and contrasts. Return to your image. Arrange and re-arrange your words to express what the text means to you. When you are satisfied with your design stick everything in place.
- Return to the text: How has engaging with the passage visually been a portal for deeper understanding? What are the implications for your life and your creativity?

## Eyes to see God

Paul urges the Colossian Christians to see that because Jesus is the image of the invisible God there is definitively nothing more to disclose—he is the "new creative act of God towards man,"[2] and from him flows creativity. Even for the disciples living alongside Jesus this was a difficult concept and one which caused Philip to ask, "Lord, show us the Father, and we will be satisfied," to which Jesus replied: "Whoever has seen me has seen the Father" (John 14:9). The writer of John's Gospel, in Eugene Peterson's paraphrase, states: "The Word became flesh and blood, and moved into the neighborhood."[3] Having the human and divine Jesus living "next door" or "down the street" brings a different dimension to the relationship, something of which is captured in a portion of liturgy from the Divine Office.

> Invisible in his own nature,
>
> God, in his great love,
>
> became visible in ours.
>
> Beyond our grasp,
>
> in his great love,
>
> he chose to come
>
> within our grasp.
>
> —St. Leo the Great[4]

Trevor Hart, who has written much on art and theology, suggests that the enfleshment of the Word, in the humanity of Jesus, is a response to the creative word of God spoken at creation. The opening verses of Psalm 19 describe how creation pours forth speech to proclaim God's glory throughout the world and Hart suggests that "God's speaking . . . is intended to elicit some response from the human side," and that the Word itself "has become human and . . . incorporated the response to itself within itself, becoming the one human in whose life a fitting response and correspondence to God's speaking may be seen."[5] Jesus was the answer to Philip's question. Being like Christ we share the capacity to respond to God with all that we are and with all the "stuff" associated with being human. In his letter to the Ephesians Paul anticipates the rich insights available to them in Christ.

2. Nichols, *The Art of God Incarnate*, 36.

3. Peterson, *The Message*, 1916.

4. https://www.catholicculture.org/culture/library/view.cfm?recnum=147.

5. Hart, cited in Begbie, *Beholding the Glory*, 17.

I pray that the God of our Lord Jesus Christ, the Father of glory, may give you a spirit of wisdom and revelation as you come to know him, so that, with the eyes of your hearts enlightened, you may know what is the hope to which he has called you . . . ." (Eph 1:17–18)

## Light and knowing

The word *light* embedded in en*light*en reminds us of the connection between seeing and understanding. The opposite, darkness, equated with spiritual blindness, is much warned about in the Bible: "Those who walk during the day do not stumble because they see the light of this world. But those who walk at night stumble, because the light is not in them" (John 11:9–10). So, how do the arts make a space for renewed understanding? The German artist Max Beckmann, argued that the arts "get hold of the invisible, [and can] penetrate, as deeply as possible into the visible."[6] Things that are unseen such as ideas, impressions, or concepts can be worked out and brought to life in one, two, or three dimensions, in movement, sound, performance, or in myriad expressive forms. We noted earlier that Jesus' incarnation was the response to the creative word spoken at creation so, in our humanity, we too can re-create, discover, and respond to God, who "is not threatened by human activity in the world but who desires our active participation in his purposes for a world which has not yet reached its final goal."[7]

> The appearing of a supreme image throws open the way for the creation of theological art apt to serve as exegesis of this new situation of the embodied disclosure of God in man. If God has elected to show himself definitively in the form of human life, then may not the artist shape and fashion visual images which will add up to an exegesis of revelation?[8]

Simply put, there is scope for discovery and exploration in art-making. For example, as we consider and re-consider papers for collage, or as we build and re-build in clay, our choices inform our learning about God

6. Beckmann, cited in *The Art of God Incarnate*, 12.

7. Hart, cited in *Beholding the Glory*, 18.

8. Nichols, *The Art of God Incarnate*, 48.

and others. It is as much through the *process* as via the final result that we uncover things not known at the outset.

At the start of his project French-Tunisian artist eL Seed did not anticipate the effects of his calligraffiti mural in the Coptic Christian Community of Manshiyat Naser in Egypt. His style fuses Arabic calligraphy with imagery in messages that are particular to a context, yet universal in meaning. This specific area is where the city of Cairo's garbage is dumped and both the town it and its inhabitants have a reputation for filth and extreme odor. Here is where pig-breeders and others sort through trash on a daily basis and where *Perception* (2016)[9] is painted on the surfaces of fifty buildings. Calligraffiti literally brings the word into the neighborhood. Also of spiritual significance is the fact that the image can only be made sense of when seen from the Monastery of St. Simon the Tanner on Moqattam Mountain. Viewed from this place of faith, hewn into the mountain side, the Arabic calligraphy and swirling blocks of color align to reveal the words of third-century Bishop Athanasius, "Anyone who wants to see the sunlight clearly needs to wipe his eye first."[10]

**Figure 13:** *Perception*
**by eL Seed, 2016**

9. www.ted.com.

10. Saint Athanasius, *On The Incarnation*, 96.

The artist reflects, "If you want to see the real image of someone, maybe you should change your angle."[11] Inviting people to adjust their perspective in order to see true humanity was a thread through the earthly ministry of Jesus. It was the personal experience of Zacchaeus, of those watching Jesus make marks in the dust, and also the subject of many parables. Seeing through the lens of the light of Christ is described by Aidan Nichols:

> It is the splendour of the divine meaning shining in the form of Christ that moves us, transforming our sensibility and habitual vision of things. Only so we can come to "image" that face of God in Jesus by a responding love, ourselves transfigured by his grace.[12]

Nichols suggests that the light of Jesus is capable of changing the way we see because as we respond in love our vision is modified. He suggests that a loving, grace-filled relationship changes "the powers of perception and lets us see the world in a way we never have before."[13] The experience of working together to pour out painted words and images onto the sides of homes revealed the image of Christ in a community steeped in garbage. In other words, "what is revealed has been there all the time, but it has gone unnoticed in our humdrum everyday experience."[14] This is Athanasius's wiping of the eye.

The inhabitants of Manshiyat Naser spoke of the fresh way in which they are now perceived as a result of the project. "You brought light to us," they insisted. However, the artist showed them that, in fact, *they* had brought the light which he demonstrated by using white glow-in-the dark paint for the calligraphy. "The goal," said el Seed "was to leave something for that community. The art will eventually disappear but perceptions were changed." This is a theme which is developed further in chapter 8.

## Reflect

As we think more about imagery and words, consider this quotation by Eugene Peterson.

> Language [is] given to us to glorify God, to receive the revelation of God, to witness to the truth of God, to offer praise to God. . . .

11. www.ted.com.

12. Nichols, *The Art of God Incarnate*, 146.

13. Ibid., 119.

14. Begbie, *Beholding the Glory*, xii.

My concern is that we use God's gift of language in consonance with the God who speaks. Jesus is the primary person with whom we have to do in this business. Jesus most of all. Jesus, the Word made flesh. Jesus who "spoke and it came to be" (Ps 33:9) even since the foundation of the world (Matt 13:35).[15]

- Does the treatment of Athanasius' text ("Anyone who wants to see the sunlight clearly needs to wipe his eye first") give glory to God? How?

- How do you receive or experience the revelation of God through eL Seed's *Perception*?

- In your own work, how are you thinking about word and image? How does the visual language you are using witness to the truth of God and offer him praise?

## Pointing to the divine—art and de-familiarization

The mystery of the incarnation, like the conception of Christ, has long offered a challenge to artists; a fact borne out by visits to national art galleries, especially in the West, where the nativity is a common theme. Contemporary artists, however, remain drawn to the subject of Christ. Why should paintings and sculptures be such prolific and often powerful carriers of this theme? "Art is important to theology," says Deborah Sokolove, "because it grounds us in the material and in the incarnational reality of what it means to be human on the earth."[16] As we use tools and shape matter we discover, as we look closely we are provoked to ask questions, to grapple, to re-visit preconceptions. But is there anything new to say? Any further visual comment to make? In the following group of paintings we will see how treatments of the subject of the nativity can transport us from well-worn Christmas card motifs to dynamic, fresh interpretations that ignite the imagination, de-familiarise the theme, and offer new insights.

In *Incarnation*, a non-figurative painting, we notice the lavish gold and red theatre flats like columns which frame the stage set into which the event of Christ's coming and ensuing scenes will unfold. This is a statement of welcome with color and lines appropriate to the King of Kings. In contrast, on the back-drop the non-linear fragmented marks and muted tones speak of the historical brokenness and groaning of creation into which

15. Peterson, *Tell it Slant*, 2.
16. Burgess, "Our Lady of Perpetual Exhaustion."

Christ stepped to offer saving grace to the world (John 3:17). While this image does not reference Luke's infancy narrative in figurative ways, there is a parallel with the star whose extraordinary brightness drew so many to worship him. The radiant theatre spotlight projected from above speaks more to the prologue of John's Gospel: "The light shines in the darkness, and the darkness did not overcome it" (John 1:5). The light fixes our gaze and we are no longer mere viewers of a painting.

**Figure 14:** *Incarnation*
**by G. C. Sakakini, 2007, textile (5' x 4.5')**

The viewer's proximity to the slanted black and white triangles suggest we have been given good seats for this play which offer an opportunity to participate. From our tiered seating we are drawn in as the audience who witnesses the light. The painting poses a question: Where do we sit in relationship to the light who is the protagonist, (main character)? Are we watching indifferently from the side? Are we leaning forward on the edge of our seats? As mentioned earlier, responding to the light is a theme that preoccupies the writer of John's Gospel (John 1:10–13). As we receive the light our story is picked up and we, as children of God, find our place in the much "bigger" narrative.

## Reflect

Spend a few moments looking at this print by Chris Stoffel Overvoorde.

**Figure 15:** *Glory Amen*
**by Chris Overvoorde, Woodcut, 2016**

As in *Incarnation* above, the heart of what is to be communicated is right at the center. The combination of curvy and straight linear marks guide our eyes through a centrifugal frame to the doves whose beaks direct us unmistakably to the Christ child. At the beginning of the chapter we noted how the coming of Christ is located at a pivotal point in the big story and we imagined the eagle symbolizing John hovering over the event of the incarnation. *Glory Amen* suspends the coming between consummation and creation through visual references and circular form. In his collection, *Revelation*, Ned Bustard writes:

> In a poem titled "On the Morning of Christ's Nativity," John Milton wrote, "That Glorious Form . . . forsook the courts of everlasting day, and chose with us a darksome house of mortal clay." In this print the artist wanted to attempt to capture the idea of the Incarnation as well as the pain and suffering of childbirth. The second person of the Trinity came into the world through a birth canal just like everyone. The twenty-four elders and the four beasts mentioned in Revelation 19:4 are here along with the seven-fold Spirit—and an *in utero* infant. Bono of U2 writes: "The Christmas story has a crazy good plot with an even crazier premise—the idea goes, if there is a force of love and logic behind the universe, then how amazing would it be if that incomprehensible power chose to express itself as a child born in shit and straw poverty."[17]

Scottish visual artist and sculptor David Mach included his collage entitled *The Nativity* (Florence) in the "Precious Light" exhibition in 2011, which celebrated the 400th anniversary of the King James Bible that year. Find this image online and take a long look so you don't miss any detail.[18]

- How does Mach's piece de-familiarise the Nativity?
- What questions does the work ask?
- What is the effect of setting the scene in Florence?

In different ways all three images show how art earths Christ's coming, how it provokes us to see things differently. "What might Jesus have to say to us today?" asks writer Ryan Dueck. "Don't be embarrassed by the particularly of God's coming to you. Don't be ashamed of the God who comes as a squalling baby boy in the manure and stench . . . don't be surprised that God's coming involves you in a story not of your choosing."[19]

17. Bustard, *Revealed*, 148.

18. For further information see https://./www/google.co.uk/amo/s/thejesusquestion. org.2015/05/06/david-mach-collages-for-sale/amp?client=safari and https:/_/_goo.gl/ images/78reKh.

19 Dueck, "The Plot We Find Ourselves In," n.p.

## Creating in the light of Christ

During this chapter we have explored ways in which our seeing is affected by the coming to earth of Jesus Christ. One remaining key area here is the role of the imagination, which we refer to in several chapters. In his teaching Jesus readily made use of everyday items and familiar themes in parables; mustard seeds and yeast, fig trees and coins roused curiosity in his listeners. These short bursts of teaching punctuate the Gospel narratives and reveal how tangible objects are able to function as symbols of deeper truths and point to God.

However, even well-known motifs can require effort on the part of the hearer/reader in order to make meaning. This is one role of the imagination. In the following delightful extract, writer and preacher Barbara Brown Taylor gives reasons why we need not fear the imagination and she encourages us to see beyond objects that have come our way to find deeper meaning.

> When imagination comes home and empties its pockets, of course there will be some sorting to do. Keep the cat's eye marble, the Japanese beetle wing, the red feather. . . . Jettison the bottle cap, the broken glass, the melted chocolate stuck with lint. But do not scold the imagination for bringing it all home, or for collecting it in the first place. There are no treasures without some trash, and the Holy Spirit can be trusted to go with us when we wander and to lead us back home again, with eyes far wiser for all they have seen.[20]

Let's embrace our imaginations, trusting in the discernment of the Holy Spirit.

## Make

Either

(a) take a walk and gather items that draw your attention,

or

(b) turn out the contents of a "catch-all" drawer in a garden shed, kitchen, or study.

---

20. Taylor, *The Preaching Life*, 51.

The power of an object to evoke meaning was familiar to historical painters in the still life tradition. "The meaning of a picture is never inscribed on its surface as brush-strokes are; meaning arises in the collaboration between signs (visual or verbal) and interpreters."[21]

1. Arrange your collection of objects artfully on a table or other surface as you would a still life with a strong directional light source, natural or artificial. You might add other traditional elements of a still life such as a cloth, bottle, or fruit.

2. Focus on one or two objects in the center of your still life and draw them in the center of your paper, leaving room to expand later. With a pencil draw "mindfully." For example, keep your pencil in contact with the paper at all times and move very slowly, constantly glancing back at your object. Draw what you see, not what you *think* you see! Follow the contours of each object as you focus all your attention onto it. Repeat strokes as you move over and around the surfaces. Make marks to describe texture and form. Consider the words of Eisner, a creativity theorist:

   > The Sistine Chapel can be ignored by someone in its presence; but even a mere stone can be attended to so that its aesthetic character can serve as a source of art.[22]

3. Now move outwards to include the whole arrangement. Draw conventionally, not mindfully, using pencil or charcoal to build up a line drawing. Notice the spaces between objects. What shapes do you see? Be aware of how light falls on the objects and indicate it by shading.

4. Now introduce color in paint or pastel. Keep a fresh, loose approach as you continue to focus on the objects and the space they occupy in relation to other ones. Engage all your senses in the exploration and allow them to inform your painting. What do you see, feel, hear, taste, or smell? What memories or associations are called to mind relating to these items? Are there any surprises? What are you choosing to say, to emphasize, or de-emphasize? Be imaginative in the colors you bring together or overlay.

21. Bryson, *Looking at the Overlooked*, 10.
22. Eisner, *The Arts and the Creation of Minds*, 10.

Reflect theologically on your image

- How are objects changed by the effect of light? Turn your image in different directions as you explore this.

- Contemplate your image with the "eyes of your heart."[23] Is there anything in the objects, your interpretation, or the process, that points you to God in a symbolic way?

- Using your fully baptized imagination as a springboard, what do you know about God that you did not know at the outset of this activity?

- Share your reflections with others.

23. See Christine Valters Paintner's book *Eyes of the Heart: Photography as a Christian Contemplative Practice.*

## chapter 6

# Cross and Comeback

As we enter the narrative of the passion, resurrection, and ascension of Jesus Christ let's pause to see where we have come from. The Creator God's intention was always to fulfill his whole creation's potential and to bring it to perfection. There was no plan B. God "[t]ook the responsibility for creating this world knowing he had the power and love to redeem it."[1] Since chapter 1 we have seen God's creative pulse at work. We recall God speaking creation into being, providing a garden to be tended and stones to be mined, and inviting Adam to participate in naming activities. We also saw the fracturing of that shalom life through a de-creative task signifying the broken relationship between God and mankind.

In chapter 3, "Calling," we looked at what makes us truly human and how our God-given vocation draws us further into God's creative purposes. The paintings below, taken together, nudge the story on from "Conception," when we planted seeds to acknowledge his creative growth at work in us, to the subject of this chapter. The theme of seeds continues. *Eclat*, the French word for "burst," describes the fullness of what the seeds have become, in that the flowering background parallels Mary's open heart towards God's call. After having processed the various stages of the angel Gabriel's message, this post-annunciation moment captures her whole embodied and exuberant "yes!"

---

1. Greenslade, *The Big Story*, 663.

**Figure 16:** *Eclat*
by Gill C. Sakakini, 6' x 5', 2016

**Figure 17:** *Réfléchie*
by Gill C. Sakakini, 6' x 5', 2016

69

However, in order that the redemptive work of Christ may take place, something needs to die first, and in *Réfléchie* (French for *reflective/pensive*) the background flowers have become dried seed pods. The crisis sin brought meant humanity needed more than a little fine-tuning here and there; it needed transformation. Just as a seed must die—be split open—for new life to emerge, so something has to die in humanity. "God split the life of His Son," says Oswald Chambers, "that the world might be saved."[2] The writer of John's Gospel underscores this—"Very truly, I tell you, unless a grain of wheat falls into the earth and dies, it remains just a single grain; but if it dies, it bears much fruit" (John 12:24). Amid joy and pain the old priest Simeon prophesies to Mary that "a sword will pierce your own soul too" (Luke 2:35), and it is on this that the vulnerable, human mother reflects in this image.[3] Yet her gaze leads out from the painting and beyond, hinting at the resurrection of her son, just as the dead pods contain all that is needed for new birth.

## A dynamic descent and ascent

The falling of the grain and the rising to new life trace the contours of Jesus' journey downwards through his death on the cross, followed by his journey upwards through his comeback from death, and his final return to the Father at his ascension. Graham Tomlin suggests that this "U-shaped" movement down and up corresponds to Christ's work of mediating, perfecting, offering, and blessing. Paul's words in Philippians 2:7–9 speak of this movement in terms of Christ's self-emptying and God exalting him.

For example, recall the descending spotlight of the incarnate Jesus from the previous chapter. Jesus enters our space "uniting human nature with himself, taking identification to the point of the cross."[4] At the lowest part in his death, as priest and mediator, "Christ stands between God and his Creation, so that the two are united in a deep intimacy . . . bringing God to us and representing us to God."[5] Next, in an upward movement through the resurrection, Christ is perfecting creation and humanity, enabling it "to become all that it was intended to be. As such, Christ brings the blessing of God to bear on his Creation. Creation comes into being in the beginning,

2. Chambers, cited in Rees-Larcombe, *A Years's Journey with God*, 202.
3. For a fuller commentary on these paintings see Appendix 5.
4. Tomlin, *The Widening Circle*, 48.
5. Ibid., 48.

yet needs the continual divine blessing for it to become all that it has the potential to be."[6] Christ then gathers all in an offering back to God, which is received as worship. The tip of this upward swing describes Jesus' ascension to be seated at his Father's right hand, and in this, "God does something new with and for the man Jesus, as a basis of that which he intends ultimately to do with and for us."[7] In the rest of this chapter we will explore through text and image what it means to create in light of the movement described above; how we might move towards fulfilling our creative potential; offer what we create; and ask God to deliver it as blessing to others.

## Read

> From noon on, darkness came over the whole land until three in the afternoon. And about three o'clock Jesus cried with a loud voice, "Eli, Eli, lema sabachthani?" that is, "My God, my God, why have you forsaken me?" When some of the bystanders heard it, they said, "This man is calling for Elijah." At once one of them ran and got a sponge, filled it with sour wine, put it on a stick, and gave it to him to drink. But the others said, "Wait, let us see whether Elijah will come to save him." Then Jesus cried again with a loud voice and breathed his last. At that moment the curtain of the temple was torn in two, from top to bottom. The earth shook, and the rocks were split. The tombs also were opened, and many bodies of the saints who had fallen asleep were raised. After his resurrection they came out of the tombs and entered the holy city and appeared to many. Now when the centurion and those with him, who were keeping watch over Jesus, saw the earthquake and what took place, they were terrified and said, "Truly this man was God's Son!" Many women were also there, looking on from a distance; they had followed Jesus from Galilee and had provided for him. Among them were Mary Magdalene, and Mary the mother of James and Joseph, and the mother of the sons of Zebedee. (Matt 27:45–56)

## Respond

List words in the passage that evoke the senses (darkness, torn, etc.). How do they build up a picture of desolation? How does the cross express the

6. Ibid., 48.

7. Farrow, quoted in Tomlin, *The Widening Circle*, 44.

fragmenting impact of sin? When, like the disciples, have you felt bereft? Stay with these words and explore them visually with different textures and patterns. You might like to look at the Bath Abbey Diptychs for ideas, particularly *Jesus Crucified* (No. 29). It might be helpful to think of ways to explain these words to someone who does not share your language.

## Discuss

Where in your creative pursuits do you experience discouragement or little "deaths," and how do you deal with them? Spend some moments considering seedpods and how they might speak of creative dry times, blocks, absence of ideas, or longing.

## Read

> After the sabbath, as the first day of the week was dawning, Mary Magdalene and the other Mary went to see the tomb. And suddenly there was a great earthquake; for an angel of the Lord, descending from heaven, came and rolled back the stone and sat on it. His appearance was like lightning, and his clothing white as snow. For fear of him the guards shook and became like dead men. But the angel said to the women, "Do not be afraid; I know that you are looking for Jesus who was crucified. He is not here; for he has been raised, as he said. Come, see the place where he lay. Then go quickly and tell his disciples, 'He has been raised from the dead, and indeed he is going ahead of you to Galilee; there you will see him.' This is my message for you." So they left the tomb quickly with fear and great joy, and ran to tell his disciples. Suddenly Jesus met them and said, "Greetings!" And they came to him, took hold of his feet, and worshiped him. Then Jesus said to them, "Do not be afraid; go and tell my brothers to go to Galilee; there they will see me." (Matt 28:1–12)

## Reflect

- Again, be aware of words in the passage that evoke the senses, also note repeated words. What is the relationship between seeing and fear in this passage?

**Figure 18:** *The Earthquake* (1st Station of the Resurrection)
**by Richard Caemmerer, 2' x 4', 2010**

- As you contemplate the image above, think about how the artist uses line and space to engage with the themes of seeing and fear? Does this alter your own perspective, if so, how?

- In your creative process do you notice a connection between seeing and fear? How do you navigate this?

- Imagine you are one of the shadowy bystanders, and, using the words from your list and insights you have had, pray for creative break-through, emerging ideas, and for ways to overcome fear.

## Read

Then he led them out as far as Bethany, and, lifting up his hands, he blessed them. While he was blessing them, he withdrew from them and was carried up into heaven. And they worshiped him, and returned to Jerusalem with great joy; and they were continually in the temple blessing God. (Luke 24:50–53)

Reflect

Meditate on the image below in light of the above.[8]

**Figure 19:** *Ascension* (17th Station of the Resurrection)
by Richard Caemmerer 2010.

8. For artist details, see Appendix 5.

## Cross, comeback, and imaginative possibilities

One of the results of holding together the despair of the cross, the joy of the resurrection, and the blessing of the ascension is that they bring fresh scope for the Christian imagination. According to William Dyrness:

> It is the teaching of Scripture . . . that in the death and resurrection of Christ something was altered in the creative order that has opened up new worlds of human possibility. Theologians call this event redemption, and it is important that we understand exactly what this means—for I believe it provides the key to the Christian imagination. Redemption is the divine process whereby the created order is restored and renewed according to the original creative purpose of God.[9]

These events have fuelled the imagination of artists and writers since the early church, though the crucified Christ was considered too raw and unfit a subject after crucifixion was forbidden by Constantine I. In spite of, or perhaps because of this constraint, artists plumbed creative depths to find symbolic ways to show the death of Christ, such as the motif of Jonah in the belly of the whale, signifying Christ in the cold, dark tomb for three days before emerging, thereby suggesting the resurrection.

As the title of this chapter suggests, the death, bodily resurrection, and subsequent ascension of Christ, although separate events, are pivotal to the salvation story and cannot be seen in isolation from each other. Paul states in Romans 5:10, "For if while we were enemies, we were reconciled to God through the death of his Son, much more surely, having been reconciled, will we be saved by his life."

Their centrality is illustrated in the early Christian monogram, the Chi-Rho, which is formed by the intersection of the first two capital letters of the word for Christ in Greek (X and P), and surrounded by a wreath, evocative of a transformed crown of thorns. The X is the symbol for the cross, which holds this image, and indeed all things, together as we noted earlier in Colossians 1.

9. Dyrness, *The Christian Imagination*, 84–94.

**Figure 20: Fourth-century sarcophagus of Domitilla in Rome**

As for visual interpretations of the resurrection, however, like the conception of Christ, its very mystery means that fewer representations exist. That said, many paintings and sculptures show the *effects* of the resurrection, particularly on those who come upon the risen Christ in the Gospels, which are the subject of "The Stations of the Resurrection". Although less frequently seen than the Stations of the Cross, artists are increasingly engaging with the various personal and corporate encounters with Jesus recorded in the Gospels. This makes a strong visual connection between the events of sombre Holy Week, the devastation and desolation of Good Friday and Holy Saturday, and the joy-filled event of Easter and the subsequent season.

## Reflect

Read the following quotation by William Dyrness:

The New Testament sees the potential that is now opened up for mankind as something so astonishing that it dares call what Christ has done a "new creation" (2 Cor 5:17). Moreover, it is clear that this new order will one day include the whole universe in its purview (Eph 1:10). To accomplish this, of course, God will have to intervene one final time to finish what was begun with Christ's death and resurrection. But clearly this new reality is already present in the world—the Resurrection itself and the gift of the Holy Spirit are evidences for this—and we can share in this transforming reality by repentance and faith in Christ. People dream of changing the world; in Christ God gives us the model and motive for such change.[10]

1. In the natural world, where do you see death or signs of death?

2. Where do you see effects of the resurrection in your life and experience?

3. What potential does art (your own or others') have to acknowledge the reality of death *and* to point to hope, redemption, reconciliation, and even changing the world?

## Meeting the God of healing and transformation in the altarpiece

Nowhere are the images of Christ's cross and comeback more central than at the table of the Eucharist, which was, for the early church father St. John Chrysostom, "a place of awe and shuddering."[11] For Thomas Aquinas, a scholastic theologian and philosopher, the eucharistic elements were "the sensible sign of the invisible cause, God,"[12] meaning something tangible that speaks powerfully of the unseen author of all things. Participation in the sensory, sacramental act of receiving the body and blood of Christ was heightened, for the medievals, by the visual impact of panel paintings behind the altar. Multiple sections were hinged together to create "wings" that literally unfolded the story, though not chronologically, causing the viewer to be drawn into a three-dimensional sacred space. Theologian Ulrich Luz comments on art's capacity to carry a story in this way: "Texts narrate a temporal sequence of events, whereas painters fill a given space."[13] Faced

10. Ibid.
11. Giles, *Here I am,* 78.
12. Viladesau, *The Beauty of the Cross,* 128.
13. Luz, *Perspectives on the Passion,* 15.

with various scenes at once we are curious and have to work to make sense of the images. This is an example of the interrogative aspect of art: images that ask questions.

The artist Matthias Grünewald filled his famous Isenheim Altarpiece with multiple scenes of the life of Christ, with the larger central panel graphically portraying the crucified and deeply suffering Jesus. Why such a depiction? In fact, the work was commissioned for a hospital room in St. Anthony's Monastery where sufferers wasted away with a debilitating skin disease, causing intense pain and social segregation. Gazing on this image and sharing visually in something of Christ's own loneliness, agony, and humanity, may have brought solace as death approached.

Figure 21: Isenhiem Altarpiece (first view, Crucifixion)
by Matthias Grünewald, 1512–16,
Unterlinden Museum, Colmar

Figure 22: Isenhiem Altarpiece (second view, Resurrection)
by Matthias Grünewald, 1512–16,
Unterlinden Museum, Colmar

Travelling through the panels we may find ourselves asking questions too about the artist's treatment of the resurrection. What is he saying about the resurrection through this light, almost over-exposed portrayal? He chooses to emphasize the *effects* of redemption on creation as well as humanity. For example, by depicting the radiating sun, whose sphere suggests the universe, he points to renewal of the entire cosmos. Jesus rises gracefully from the black background of death and our gaze follows; similarly participants are invited to lift up their hearts before the altar, indicating also the final movement of the ascension. "The Lord's Supper tells the story of Jesus of Nazareth, and at the same time it points us, indeed pulls us, upwards to the risen Christ. If we can embrace this more fully, our knowledge of Christ will broaden and deepen."[14] As the following suggests, this expands the realms of possibility for making.

> Grünewald is an expressionist often seemingly obsessed with the tragedy of man. Yet he has caught perhaps more precisely than any other artist the glory of creation in the light of the incarnate Christ and the transfiguration of matter in the light of the resurrected Christ.[15]

With the coming back of Christ from the dead a whole new order for both humanity and creation emerges. It looks nothing like the old one. And God's wisdom is at the center of it, a kind of wisdom that seems foolish to those who reject the cross.

When Christ submitted himself to death on the cross, it is as if he, as the representative of the human race, had taken all of that old, weary, conflict-ridden existence, with the inevitability of constant friction and strife, and plunged it into the cold tomb. The old humanity, marked by division and conflict had died. And then the miracle had taken place: a new humanity had arisen.[16]

## Re-making and offering

Staying with the theme of the table or altar, in the final part of this chapter we look at the implications of the new humanity for making. "Whether through paint or sound, metaphor or movement, we are given the inestimable gift of participating in the re-creative work of the Triune God," states Jeremy Begbie, "anticipating that final and unimaginable re-creation of all matter, space, and time, the fulfilment of all things visible and invisible."[17] This hopeful and exciting vision is worked out through broken lives receiving the broken body of Christ and being transformed by the outpouring of his blood. Having been fed, we are sent out again in the power of the Holy Spirit who works with the one who shapes and re-shapes individuals and communities.

Look at the images below of the Keiskamma Altarpiece[18] made by 130 women in Hamburg, South Africa in 2005 using embroidery, appli-

---

14. Collicutt, *The Psychology of Christian Character Formation*, 25.

15. Dixon, *Images of Redemption*, 75.

16. Tomlin, *Looking Through the Cross*, 176.

17. Begbie, quoted in David Taylor, *For the Beauty of the Church*, 181.

18. Keiskamma art project, a programme of Keiskamma Trust www.keiskamma.org.

qué, and photographs. The community, overwhelmed by the HIV/Aids epidemic, created this altarpiece under the direction of doctor and artist Carol Hofmeyr who engaged people in facing the reality of death and acknowledging the hope of resurrection through art. Each panel depicts real members of the community, many of whom died, some of whom were grandmothers, all honored for unique roles. As they were making the altarpiece, long-awaited antiretroviral drugs were released to sufferers, which brought resurrection hope into their midst.

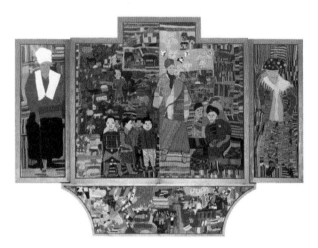

**Figure 23: Keiskamma Altarpiece, first view, Crucifixion, (4.15 x 6.8 metres), 2004**

**Figure 24: Keiskamma Altarpiece, second view, Resurrection (4.15 x 6.8 metres), 2004**

- How might community have been re-shaped by this collaborative project?

- Works of art can be described as having *"after-lives,"* which refers to art's capacity to project meaning forward into a contemporary time-frame. How do you "receive" this art in the present tense in your own context?

## Our making

Looking at the following images and final poem, consider how your own creative project can be an offering to others. For example, the communion table[19] below declares, "He is not here—He is risen!" inviting all to enter, receive, and go through the opening.

**Figure 25: Communion Table and Lectern
by Stephen Owen, the chapel, Guildford Baptist Church**

The artist, Stephen Owen, writes about creating from imperfection:

God's power, God's design, God's ways go far beyond what we know and see. As creator of all things his fingerprints are

19. For more details see Appendix 5 or for information about the artist go to http://www.stephenowen.com.

everywhere—even the everyday materials we use come from him. In life we all experience unexpected events. I believe this furniture would not have taken on the form it has if I had not experienced brokenness. Whilst we try to avoid pain of any sort, God, in his loving ways is always with us and leads us through these times to make us more like him. Let the stories of our lives bring glory to him!

Finally, and appropriately, the altar in the Cathedral of St. Julien in Le Mans, France points to future creativity. Dramatic gold light fractures the effects of sin and death, but the markings on the stone speak of human flesh. In the new heavens and the new earth what might creativity look like? The poet, Michael Symmons Roberts, imagines its ongoing process with more making and naming to be done!

**Figure 26:** *L'Autel*
**by Daniel Bonhommet**

*Food for Risen Bodies—VI*

(Abeja blanca zumbas—ebria de miel—en mi alma—Pablo Neruda)

No longer ravenous, they smoke
and sip. Some carry tables out

to get a feel for sun on skin again.
More words are coming back,

so there's a lot of naming.
Old ones still hold good—*oak,*

*brook, crab, sycamore*—but more
are needed now. They mull

potential titles for these new
white bees, as sharp as stars

against the ivories of cherry
or magnolia. Word gets round

the bees were new creations
made in honour of a poet,

so they wait for him to choose.
He's in no hurry, cups them

in his hands, weighs up the tenor
of their hum. The sun brings colour

to the diners' sallow skins.
Although these bodies were not

theirs before, there are resemblances,
and flesh retains a memory

even beyond death, so every
lover's touch, each blow or cut

is rendered into echo not the hand,
the lips, the neck. Some fall silent,

while their own phenomenology
is mapped across them.

Others look astonished,
expecting their new skin to be

a blank sheet, but the man
who went ahead to find a route

for them came back with wounds
intact and palpable. No pain,

but a record nontheless, a history
of love and war in blank tattoos.[20]

## Discuss

- The words of Oswald Chambers at the beginning of this chapter close with this challenge: "God split the life of His Son that the world might be saved; are we prepared to spill out our lives for Him?"[21]
- What might it look like to pour out our creativity for Christ as an offering, as Mary did with the alabaster jar of perfume? (Mark 14:3). What could be the cost for you?
- The cross is not the last word in the story. The resurrection-ascension is. "In that sense, the cross is something of a semi-colon not a full stop.[22] . . . Christian faith believes, against all intuition and instinct, that death ends in life."[23] What difference does the resurrection make to our creativity?

20. Roberts, *Corpus*, 61.

21. Chambers, cited in Rees-Larcombe, *A Year's Journey with God*, 202.

22 A "full stop" is the British phrase for a period at the end of a sentence.

23. Tomlin, *Looking Through the Cross*, 198.

This life is not a dress rehearsal, but perhaps it's not the whole story. For one day Christ will return. The cross of Christ and the resurrection cannot be separated—one day we too will be raised. All that is promised in Christ will find its completion one day, when we see him face to face. He is the "Morning Star" for whom we wait. As C. S. Lewis writes: "We discern the freshness and purity of morning"[24]—yet for the moment it's just a hint of what's to come. We still see much that is painful and broken in the world, "[b]ut all the leaves of the New Testament are rustling with the rumour that it will not always be so."[25]

## Make

*A new creation: fragments mosaic*

For this task you will be invited to participate in a guided group activity, however, if you are not following the course with others please see the Leader's Guide for chapter 6.

## Reflect

As you prepare to make during the group session, spend some moments in confession.

- Unless we recognize the brokenness inside ourselves, and our world, we cannot enter into the wholeness of Christ. And ultimately to follow Christ is to know his death and share in his brokenness, as well as his resurrection. Our lives are shaped by the cross of Jesus.

- In the de-creative task of tile breaking we named before God the fragments that represented fractured pieces of our lives. Now lay those fractured pieces down around the cross in recognition that it is only through his death that new life can come.

24. Lewis, *The Weight of Glory*, 43.
25. Ibid., 43.

## chapter 7

# Charisma

## Inspiration

Have you ever wondered why it is that so many artists resort to spirits—be they in the form of alcohol, drugs, or some kind of muse—in order to make their art? It might be a cliché, but clichés tend to exist because they are well-worn truths. The need for inspiration from outside oneself seems to have been experienced by generations of artists. Classically, inspiration came in the form of the muse, who was believed to stir the artist or poet with fresh insights. Lee Siegel describes the muse as "a gust of divine wind that blew through the human vessel lucky enough to be graced by her attention."[1] Often the muse was represented by a female, kept tantalizingly out of reach. Today the desire for the muse may have thinned out—along with the number of women prepared to play valet to someone else's imagination![2] However, the artist's need for inspiration remains.

At the start of the third millennium, John Paul II wrote the following letter to artists:

> Dear artists,
>
> You well know that there are many impulses which, either from within or from without, can inspire your talent. Every genuine

1. Siegal, "Where Have All the Muses Gone?"
2. Ibid. Siegel attributes this to several trends in our culture, one of them being individualism and another being a growing rejection of the objectification of women.

inspiration, however, contains some tremor of that "breath" with which the Creator Spirit suffused the work of creation from the very beginning. . . . [H]e awakens energies of mind and heart which enable it to conceive an idea and give it form in a work of art. It is right then to speak, even if only analogically, of "moments of grace. . . ."[3]

The letter is entitled, "The Creator Spirit and Artistic Inspiration." Often in our liturgies the Holy Spirit is invoked in relation to creativity: *"Veni, Creator Spiritus . . ."* (Come, Creator Spirit . . .). As Christian makers we look not to a human muse, nor to addictive substances, but to the Creator Spirit for inspiration: the Holy Spirit.

This Spirit forms part of the triune Godhead and is a person, as Rublev's icon reminded us in the introduction. Hendrikus Berkhof defines the Holy Spirit as "the personal God himself in relation to us."[4] This chapter will explore the relationship between the Holy Spirit and our making.

## Charisms

The New Testament speaks of the Holy Spirit as both promised "gift" to all those who repent and are baptized (Acts 2:38) and also as "the giver of gifts"—or "charisms" (1 Cor 12:4–9). Thus the Spirit builds us up. While our sense of self is often diminished by drugs and alcohol—or even a muse—the Holy Spirit *gives himself* to us, leaving us with more than we had at the start.[5] The response to the Spirit is not a Dionysian dance of madness in which the self dissolves;[6] the Holy Spirit actually builds us up, gifting us to be more truly ourselves, and brings order to what we do. For example, in Moses' day, the Spirit is there in the making of the tabernacle,[7] as we shall see later on, filling Bezalel, the master craftsman, "with wisdom, with understanding, with knowledge and with all kinds of skill—to make artistic designs for work in gold, silver, and bronze, to cut and set stones, to work in wood, and to engage in all kinds of crafts" (Exod 31:3–5).

---

3. "The Creator Spirit and Artistic Inspiration," From *Letter of John Paul II to Artists.*

4. Berkhof, *The Doctrine of the Holy Spirit,* 116.

5. Guthrie, *Creator Spirit,* 116.

6. Misopolinou, *Ecstasy.* http://people.brunel.ac.uk.

7. The tent of meeting that was the symbolic dwelling-place of YHWH with Israel, a focal point for maintaining the relationship of God with his people.

We are built up, as we will see in the next chapters, not just individually, but also as the body of Christ. Paul urges the Christians of Corinth to eagerly desire the gifts or *charisms* that build up the church (1 Cor 14:26).[8] As Miroslav Volf points out: "the flow of God's gifts shouldn't stop as soon as it reaches us. The outbound movement must continue. Indeed, in addition to making us flourish, giving to others is the very purpose for which God gave us the gifts."[9]

This relationship—and all that flows from it—is completely *free*. It is all grace; we are merely gift-bearers. This means that we will view artistic gifting through a different lens from that of our celebrity culture, in which the "talented" are placed center-stage and idolized.[10] In the salvation story, there is only one who takes center-stage: Jesus Christ. Everything the Spirit does points to Christ and to his teaching (John 14:26).

The Spirit works to realize the trajectory of the salvation story, and, as Guthrie writes: "We do not discern the Spirit by running down an inspector's checklist of principles and criteria. Rather, we locate ourselves and our situation within a trajectory that originates in Eden and culminates in the New Jerusalem, and which is oriented decisively by passing through the cross."[11] The Spirit guides us into this truth (John 14:17; 16:13) and helps to refashion us in the image of Christ. As this happens, we become "image-bearers."[12]

## Images of the Spirit

Powerful images relating to the Spirit span the Testaments: the Spirit is likened to oil trickling, water flowing, fire burning, wind blowing, and breath stirring.[13] This section will explore two biblical images associated with the Spirit and will relate them to our own making.

---

8. There is, therefore, no place for the Christian maker to be narcissistic.

9. Volf, *Free of Charge,* 49.

10. Guthrie, *Creator Spirit,* 123.

11. Ibid., 167.

12. Ibid., 121.

13. Fiddes, *Participating in God,* 37.

## Wind and breath

The word for "breath" or "wind" (Hebrew: *ruach*; Greek: *pneuma*) is used regularly in the Bible to refer to the Spirit.[14] Taylor writes: "What (the disciples) had seen in Jesus and now experienced in themselves was not a new Spirit but the same dynamic and creative *ruach*, now available in that unprecedented way that the prophets had foretold."[15] We will pick up on this image of "breath" later on.

## A hovering bird

Another significant image for the Spirit, which appears in both the Old and the New Testament, is that of a bird. At the start of creation, we find the Spirit *hovering* over the chaotic waters (Gen 1:2). Robert Alter points out that the verb "hover" attached to God's Spirit here is the same verb used to describe an eagle fluttering over its young in the Old Testament, and it suggests parturition or nurture.[16] The Gospel of Luke contains several references to the Spirit being present at significant times in the life of Jesus. As we have seen, the Spirit is there in the annunciation (Luke 1:35); the Spirit descends on Jesus like a dove at his baptism (Luke 3:22); and then leads—or drives—Jesus into the wilderness where he is tested (Luke 34:1). Interestingly, however, the Spirit is not explicitly present in the Gospel accounts of the crucifixion.[17] Into this vacuum, William Blake sketches an exchange that we imagine was longed for as Christ hung on the cross.[18]

---

14. Sherry, *Spirit and Beauty*, 5, 83.

15. Taylor, *The Go Between God*, 85–86.

16. Alter, *The Five Books of Moses*, 17.

17  In fact, in Matthew and Mark's Gospels, Jesus expresses his sense of abandonment in those well-known words, "My God, my God, why have you forsaken me?" (Matt 27:46; Mark 15:34).

18. Jesus' Farewell Discourse points to this exchange in John 13–17.

**Figure 27: *The Trinity sketch*
by William Blake, c. 1793**

## Reflect

In Blake's sketch, the Spirit hovers over the Father as he embraces his crucified Son.

- Notice the wingspan of the hovering bird, representing the Spirit. What does the bird's size and shape evoke for you?

- Look at the postures of Father, Son, and Spirit in this sketch. What does this suggest about the exchange between the Trinity?

- In John's Gospel, Jesus reminds his disciples that they too can be caught up in this exchange of love between Father, Son, and Spirit (John 14:15–21).

This is a scene of deep intimacy, and the shape created by the three figures reminds us of the reciprocal love at the heart of the Trinity (See introduction). The Bible invites us to participate through our union with Christ in this divine relationship (2 Pet 1:4).

During his farewell speech, Jesus, the Son, had promised the Spirit to his disciples (John 14:15–16), and told them that the Spirit will remind them of Jesus' teaching (14:26) and testify about him (15:26). They, in turn, must testify about him too (15:27). Before his ascension, Jesus had instructed his disciples not to leave Jerusalem, but to "wait" for the baptism of the Holy Spirit (Acts 1:4–5). This is where we find them now.

## Read

When the day of Pentecost had come, they were all together in one place. And suddenly from heaven there came a sound like the rush of a violent wind, and it filled the entire house where they were sitting. Divided tongues, as of fire, appeared among them, and a tongue rested on each of them. All of them were filled with the Holy Spirit and began to speak in other languages, as the Spirit gave them ability.

Now there were devout Jews from every nation under heaven living in Jerusalem. And at this sound the crowd gathered and was bewildered, because each one heard them speaking in the native language of each. Amazed and astonished, they asked, "Are not all these who are speaking Galileans? And how is it that we hear, each of us, in our own native language? Parthians, Medes, Elamites, and residents of Mesopotamia, Judea and Cappadocia, Pontus and Asia, Phrygia and Pamphylia, Egypt and the parts of Libya belonging to Cyrene, and visitors from Rome, both Jews and proselytes, Cretans and Arabs—in our own languages we hear them speaking about God's deeds of power." All were amazed and perplexed, saying to one another, "What does this mean?" But others sneered and said, "They are filled with new wine."

But Peter, standing with the eleven, raised his voice and addressed them, "Men of Judea and all who live in Jerusalem, let this be known to you, and listen to what I say. Indeed, these are not drunk, as you suppose, for it is only nine o'clock in the morning. No, this is what was spoken through the prophet Joel:

"In the last days it will be, God declares,
   that I will pour out my Spirit upon all flesh,
   and your sons and your daughters shall prophesy,
   and your young men shall see visions,
   and your old men shall dream dreams.

> Even upon my slaves, both men and women,
> in those days I will pour out my Spirit;
> and they shall prophesy.
> And I will show portents in the heaven above
> and signs on the earth below,
> blood, and fire, and smoky mist.
> The sun shall be turned to darkness
> and the moon to blood,
> before the coming of the Lord's great and glorious day.
> Then everyone who calls on the name of the Lord shall be saved."
> (Acts 2:1–21)

## Respond

- What strikes you in this passage about the coming of the Holy Spirit?
- What does the Spirit empower the disciples to do?

## "And suddenly . . ."

It was only when Jesus was glorified, through his death and resurrection, that the Spirit was poured out. Before Jesus' death, John's Gospel states: "The Spirit had not yet been given, because Jesus had not yet been glorified" (John 7:39). Hanson translates this as "it was not yet Spirit," much as one might say, "It was not yet spring."[19]

The disciples needed to wait for this moment. Yet, as John V. Taylor points out, this kind of waiting can be a rare thing to find amongst Christians now. He writes, "I have not heard recently of committee business adjourned because those present are still awaiting the arrival of the Spirit of God. I have known projects abandoned for lack of funds, but not for the lack of the gifts of the Spirit."[20] The disciples were positioned to receive the Spirit. We need to position ourselves too—and to wait.

"And suddenly" the Holy Spirit comes. *The Message* paraphrases Acts 2:2 as, "Without warning there was a sound like a strong wind, gale force— no one could tell where it had come from." The images used to capture the

---

19. As cited in Taylor, *The Go Between God*, 85.
20. Ibid., 5.

Spirit (breath of life, tongue of fire, hovering wings, blowing winds) suggest an unpredictable and elemental energy, one that comes when it will and which cannot be controlled.[21] Like a bird, it pounces; like a rush of wind, it blows in.

## Discuss

- Have you ever experienced this "And suddenly . . ." encounter with the Holy Spirit? What happened?

- How did the encounter make you feel?

- What has it emboldened you to do?

- If you have not yet received the Holy Spirit and would like to, ask someone to pray with you.

## Tongues are loosed

Remember the story of Babel we looked at in chapter 2? Those who tried to out-create God had their language confounded. Yet here, post-resurrection, as the promised Spirit is poured out on Jesus' disciples, Babel is reversed and the language barriers are overcome. The disciples are able to reach out to the different people groups present in Jerusalem, declaring the wonders of God *in their own tongues* (Acts 2:6, 8, 11). The Holy Spirit "releases people from the prison house of language"[22] and we believe that the Spirit can be poured out today so that we speak in people's own languages through what we make. Peter tells the big salvation story in Acts 2 and, while some listeners scoff, others are stirred to question: "Amazed and perplexed, they asked one another, 'What does this mean?'" (Acts 2:12). This is our prayer for our own creative making: that our creative "tongues" would be loosed to tell the story afresh; that we would be emboldened in our telling of it; and that it would stir wonder and questions.

Interestingly, the crowd doesn't suddenly become one homogenized group, all speaking the same language. Instead, what results is a vibrant Christian community of the "unlike," energized by and keeping in step with

---

21. Ibid., 48.

22. As cited in Guthrie, *Creator Spirit*, 115. Note that this appears to be different from the use of tongues in 1 Corinthians 14, which Paul argues edifies the individual, but not the body of Christ. At Pentecost, tongues are loosed to tell the gospel story afresh.

the Spirit (Acts 2:42–47). As we saw in the introduction, God is not elitist. The coming of the Spirit does not result in a cozy club being created, from which outsiders are excluded. Quite the opposite. Outsiders, we read, are "added daily" as they are saved (Acts 2:47). This is an inclusive, dynamic, and gathering community.[23]

## Breathe on us

We saw that one image associated with the Spirit was that of "breath." In the beginning, God created *ex nihilo*—out of nothing—and after forming the man, God breathed into his nostrils "the breath of life" (Gen 2:7). The Greek word *theopneustos*, sometimes translated "inspired," literally means "God-breathed" (2 Tim 3:16) and our own word "inspiration" itself is derived from Latin meaning "breathed into" (*inspiratio*). The idea is that God breathes his own breath/Spirit into the inspired person[24]

This is a subject that Steven Guthrie has explored insightfully in his book *Creator Spirit*. He refers to Peter Shaffer's *Amadeus*, in which the composer Salieri becomes increasingly jealous of his peer, Mozart. Eventually he decides to attend Mozart's opera, *The Magic Flute*, and during the performance he asks where this divine sound could have come from. Then he turns to look at Mozart and realizes that Mozart *is* the magic flute and God the "relentless player."[25] This idea can be traced far back in the Christian tradition. Here are the *Odes of Solomon* 6:1–2:

> As the wind glides through the harp and the strings speak,
> So the Spirit of the Lord speaks through my members, and I speak
> through His love

We need this breath of life for, as we saw in chapter 1, unlike God, we have no internal resources with which to create.[26] In the words of Job:

> If he should take back his spirit (*ruach*) to himself
> and gather to himself his breath,
> all flesh would perish together
> and all mortals would return to dust. (Job 34:14–15)

23. Picasso's *La Ronde de Jeunesse* is worth looking at online at this point. The image is used on the front cover of an edition of Bonhoeffer's *Life Together* and is a good example of the dynamic, colorful, "unity-in-difference" that the Spirit brings.

24. Guthrie, *Creator Spirit*, 96.

25. Amadeus, as cited in ibid., 96.

26. Ibid., 120.

As Guthrie points out, "The human artist's business is not 'spiration'—a 'breathing forth'—but in-spiration—being breathed into."[27] This cannot be controlled. As Jesus said: "The wind blows wherever it pleases. You hear its sound, but you cannot tell where it has come from or where it is going. So it is with everyone born of the Spirit" (John 3:8). Like the disciples, our job is simply to position ourselves to receive.

## "The ministry of re-imagination"

As we saw in the chapter 3 (Calling), we are invited to partner with God in his redemptive plans for this broken world. As Walter Brueggemann states, we need new vision for familiar realities.[28] Part of the outworking of being breathed upon by the Spirit is the ability to see the world as God sees it. Stephen Guthrie calls this "the ministry of re-imagination."[29]

In the Bible, prophet-poets like Isaiah invite people to re-see reality, whether it be rulers or nations (e.g., Isa 40; Amos 6:1, 4–9; Zech 8:4–8).[30] These prophet-poets look on the same reality as everyone else but are able to reimagine it. We want to enter this ministry of re-imagination through our making so that others can gain a truer perspective on the world. Furthermore, the prophet-poets' creative acts were often performative—they actually *wrought* God's action through what they did/made—as we shall develop further in our final chapter.

This ministry of re-imagination is not synonymous with a "think positive" approach to the world. Rather, it is a prophetic voicing of God's perspective on it. This may involve a "tearing down" as well as a "building up."[31] As Paul House points out, renewal and punishment were never competing voices for the Old Testament prophets.[32] For example, in 2 Samuel 12, the prophet Nathan tells a story to help David re-see his adulterous affair with Bathsheba from God's perspective.[33] As makers, we can create works that voice God's perspective on the dis-eased parts of our world. Writing about poetry, Rowan Williams suggests that it "is not grounded in

27. Ibid., 98.
28. Brueggemann, *The Prophetic Imagination*, 3.
29. This phrase is used by Guthrie, *Creator Spirit*, 134.
30. Ibid. 135.
31. Brueggemann, *Hopeful Imagination*, 59.
32. House, "Outrageous Demonstrations of Grace," 40.
33. Guthrie, *Creator Spirit*, 171.

some celebratory sense of being at home in the world, but rather in an acute awareness of the world not being at home in itself, in a sense of *dislocation*."[34] The following examples show how a ministry of re-imagination can be used in God's redemptive plans for his world.

## Re-naming

Part of this creative ministry may involve re-naming people and places. A friend of mine who works in the Democratic Republic of the Congo as a physiotherapist noticed that many Congolese children are named according to the circumstances of their birth. For example, a child born a long way from home may be called "Safari" or "Journey." If the mother is happy at the birth of the child then a girl might be called "Faraha" in Swahili, which means "Joy" or "Neema" (Grace). A boy may be called "Agenu" (Hope). However, harder times are also often marked by the names given to the children. My friend has met children called "Suffering" ("Mateso") or "Distress" ("Taabu"), or even "Outcast" ("Makati").

As we saw in Genesis 2, Adam was invited to *name* the creatures God brought to him, and to seal their identity. Through God's covenant faithfulness, we are pulled back into God's creative purposes, this time in redemption. The Holy Spirit can help us to *re-name* people according to the way that God sees them in his redemption plan. We see an example of this in Hosea's writing. Over those who are considered "outsiders" or "forgotten," God says, "I will show love to those who are called 'Unloved,' and to those who were called 'Not-My-People' I will say, 'You are my people,' and they will answer, 'You are our God'" (Hos 2:23). In our re-imagining of the world as art-makers we can give people new names through what we make, according to the way God sees them.

For example, the photographer Sarah Bennett created a project with the Isan people sold into prostitution in Thailand. In it, she renamed the whore "sister," "daughter," and "child of God."[35] As Guthrie points out, Bennett plays Adam: "Like Adam in the garden, Sarah's camera looks out over the girls of Bangkok and says, 'Your name is "human"; your name is "beloved"; your name is "image of God."'"[36]

---

34. Williams, www.sagepublications.com.

35. See Sarah Bennett's "An Artistic Response to the Trafficking of Isan Women in Bangkok as Prostitutes" (BA hons thesis, Belmont University, Nashville, TN, 2008), as cited in Guthrie, *Creator Spirit*, 175.

36. Guthrie, *Creator Spirit*, 176.

Figure 28: *Redlight*
by Sarah Bennett

Figure 29: *Isan Innocence*
by Sarah Bennett

**Figure 30:** *Strong*
**by Sarah Bennett**

Other creative mediums can be used to re-name people. For example, a UK-based music ensemble called Epiphany tours the UK regularly, creating what they call "sound portraits." Visiting galleries, exhibitions, community projects and national events, Epiphany invites individuals or couples to sit before them and be played over. Praying before they play, the music group allows themselves to be guided by impressions that they perceive and by the Spirit. From here, they play a "sound portrait" of the person sitting before them. They might play a certain motif, chord structure, or melody, interwoven to produce a piece of music that they believe captures some aspect of that person's identity. After they have finished playing, they will speak to the person and tell them what they felt they saw.[37] The project has been very well-received and Epiphany has been invited to a wide range of venues, including art galleries, the Ideal Home Show (London), and the RHS Flower Show (Hampton Court).

37. Williamson, *Epiphany*, epiphanymusic.org.uk.

**Figure 31: "Sound Portrait"**
**by Epiphany, National Portrait Gallery, September 2014**

Epiphany also works with asylum seekers and recovering alcoholics, helping individuals see themselves through God's eyes. Some parts of the melody might contain sadness, when pain is perceived, but it will also voice notes of hope and joy. These prophet-artists do more than just see; they re-see. They call out that which God sees—and then they bless it.[38] This ministry of re-imagination happens not through lots of words but through music.

**Figure 32: "Sound Portrait"**
**by Epiphany, Manchester, February 2016**

38. A creative echo of what God does in Genesis 1.

**Figure 33: "Sound Portrait"
by Epiphany, Manchester, February 2016[39]**

## Make

1. Scan your world. Where are you aware of those who might feel "outsiders," "forgotten," or "unloved"? It could be a particular person or a community.

2. How might God see these people? How might he be asking you to re-imagine them through your creative gift? Invite the Holy Spirit to hover over your imagination and to in-spire you.

3. What creative medium would you like to use to "re-name" this person or community? It could be through photography or music, as we have seen, or some other medium, e.g., writing or visual art.

4. Get making!

5. Take a rough draft along to your group session. There will be the chance to continue working on this task, so bring any materials with you. You may wish to discuss how this "re-naming" could be offered "live" to people at the exhibition.

39. These "Sound Portraits" were made of asylum seekers at the Boaz Trust.

## chapter 8

# Community

We begin this exploration of community by casting our minds back to Mary's visit to her cousin Elizabeth from chapter 4, "Conception". In the history of art many paintings focus on the relationship between the two women as they share the excitement of Mary's news and celebrate the joy of *both* of their unexpected pregnancies. The range of visual interpretations of this moment reflects a wide variety of human interaction. For example, in *The Visitation* by Rogier van der Weyden, 1445, the artist makes the pregnancy central to the meeting by having Elizabeth's hand emphatically placed on Mary's abdomen. In a later contrasting treatment of the subject in 1894 by Maurice Denis a polite distance is kept as this sensitive and awkward news is delivered in a way that perhaps reflects the social norms of contemporary bourgeois French society.

Figure 34: *The Visitation*
by Roger van der Weyden, 1445

Figure 35: *The Visitation*
by Maurice Denis, 1894

In a third, the eighth-century "Diptych of Genoels-Elderen," we notice in the lower register of the miniature ivory panel the sculptor's choice to emphasize the close bond between the women through lines that trace and interweave from the tip of their haloes to their shared platform space. The central, symmetrical pose draws us right into the intimacy of the moment where we notice the proximity of their pressed cheeks and torsos. The curvy linear arms appear exaggerated in length, particularly Elizabeth's strong right arm, which enfolds Mary in a blessing.

**Figure 36:** *The Annunciation and the Visitation of the Virgin Mary to her cousin Elizabeth*, **ivory, (30 x 18 cm)**

Could this encounter be a picture of community? Henri Nouwen suggests that it is:

> I think *that* is the model of the Christian community. It is a community of support, celebration, and affirmation in which we can lift up what has already begun in us. The visit of Elizabeth and

Mary is one of the Bible's most beautiful expressions of what it means to form community, to be together, gathered around a promise, affirming that something is really happening.[1]

This notion of community is developed by Dietrich Bonhoeffer, who indicates that community for the Christian is created by being with just *one* other person. He states in his book *Life Together* that this person is a "physical sign of the gracious presence of the triune God."[2] Just as the waters of baptism and the bread and wine of holy communion are an "outward and visible sign of an inward and spiritual grace,"[3] so a *person* can point to God in a sacramental way and be a means of grace. Therefore, being in the company of others provides opportunities for fresh knowledge of God. When we are engaged in the process of making in the company of others, even those with different ideas, styles, and personalities (and perhaps *because* of them), we may be pointed to God through the work of their hands and their innovative suggestions. In fact, collaboration captures something of the relational life of the Trinity and celebrates unity in diversity, a topic to which we shall return later in the chapter.

## Growing together in community

Community offers a supportive and encouraging context in which ideas can continue to germinate (remember the seeds), mature, and burst forth. In community we can "lift up what has already begun in us"[4] in the service of a wider audience such as with those who will gather to share the fruit of the work of our hands at the end of this course. In fact, a different dimension is added when works of art are shared in a public space because the work is affected by the space it occupies, the light source, the context, and the generation of discussion. The poet Dylan Thomas remarked, "a poem on the page is only half a poem,"[5] suggesting that it is made complete through performance or sharing aloud. Whether this is the case or not, seeing art or hearing a poem read engages our senses, causing the art to exist in a different way because of what the viewer or listener brings to it. When

1. Nouwen, *The Only Necessary Thing*, 124. Italics mine.
2. Bonhoeffer, *Life Together*, 9.
3. https://www.churchofengland.org/prayer-worship/worship/book-of-common-prayer/a-catechism.aspx.
4. Nouwen, *The Only Necessary Thing*, 124.
5. Kelly, *Spoken Worship*, 13.

we take the brave step of putting our work out for others to see we make ourselves vulnerable, yet, as we give room for dialogue, our story intersects with other stories, which can be a rich mix. Let's look at an early practical biblical example of living and working together for followers of the "The Way" in the emerging Christian community.

## Read

They devoted themselves to the apostles' teaching and fellowship, to the breaking of bread and the prayers. Awe came upon everyone, because many wonders and signs were being done by the apostles. All who believed were together and had all things in common; they would sell their possessions and goods and distribute the proceeds to all, as any had need. Day by day, as they spent much time together in the temple, they broke bread at home and ate their food with glad and generous hearts, praising God and having the goodwill of all the people. And day by day the Lord added to their number those who were being saved. (Acts 2: 42–47)

## Read

Now the whole group of those who believed were of one heart and soul, and no one claimed private ownership of any possessions, but everything they owned was held in common. With great power the apostles gave their testimony to the resurrection of the Lord Jesus, and great grace was upon them all. There was not a needy person among them, for as many as owned lands or houses sold them and brought the proceeds of what was sold. They laid it at the apostles' feet, and it was distributed to each as any had need. (Acts 4:32–35)

## Respond

- Spend time in the text by using the practice of *visuo divina* (you will find instructions in Appendix 1).
- What actions and attitudes do you identify as potentially helpful for creative collaboration?

## Word and image in conversation

This illumination (decoration of a manuscript to bring out meaning) appears in *The Saint John's Bible*,[6] which is an extraordinary example of working together creatively on several levels. Firstly, it was commissioned in 1998 by an actual community, the Benedictine Community of Saint John's Abbey and University in Collegeville, Minnesota, and it combines the old and the new; ancient techniques done in the present. Secondly, as an entirely hand-written, hand-illuminated Bible it demonstrates collaboration between people; calligraphers and artists, led by Donald Jackson.[7] As a result, word and image weave together in a lively interplay throughout the vellum pages, each enhancing the other. Finally, *The Saint John's Bible* shows collaboration of place since work was accomplished over two continents.

**Figure 37:** *Life in Community*
by Aidan Hart and Donald Jackson, completed 2011,
pigments on vellum, (2' x 3' when open)

6. www.saintjohnsbible.org Copyright 2002, *The Saint John's Bible*, Saint John's University, Collegeville, Minnesota, USA.

7. For a comprehensive guide, see Susan Sink's volumes, *The Art of the St. John's Bible*.

*The Saint John's Bible* is a work of art and a work of theology. A team of artists coordinated by Donald Jackson in Wales and a team of scholars in Central Minnesota have brought together the ancient techniques of calligraphy and illumination with an ecumenical Christian approach to the Bible rooted in Benedictine spirituality. The result is a living document and a monumental achievement.[8]

*Life in Community* draws us back to the harmonious depiction in the passages above primarily through the choice of the colors blue and orange, which are complementary on the color wheel and when juxtaposed they mutually intensify each other. The blue looks more blue, the orange more orange. Community is also expressed in the unbroken circular design. A "rondelle" or round form in art always serves to focus the eye on what is important, which is the relationship of the centrally placed Christ to the gathered semi-circular assembly. We recall Paul's description of Jesus in Colossians, "He himself is before all things, and in him all things hold together. He is the head of the body, the church; he is the beginning, the first-born from the dead, so that he might come to have first place in everything" (Col 1:17–19). As often seen in the icon tradition, the ascended Christ is shown in an almond-shaped "mandorla," which symbolizes majesty and mystery. Luke's ideal representation of community is echoed through the ordered table, symmetrical composition, harmonious colors, and resolved circular design. Leading outward from Mary, who symbolizes the gathered church, there is a span of saints and apostles whose gestures serve to link them one to another. There are members of other countries too, such as the Middle East and Guatemala in distinctive dress which hints at diversity in community. In the lower span the common table is set with bread and wine through which the mystery of Christ is reflected and revealed from above echoing the curve of the mandorla.

In reality, of course, community is rarely so smooth and it's possible that the tumbling letters could be read as individual members. Each letter, like each human, is uniquely crafted, overlaid with precious gold, and brought into being by God the Creator. Similarly the beautifully formed shapes are delivered to the page by the steady hand of the master calligrapher. The letters find their place around the circle, jostling against each other, squeezing in to their spot. They are organic, living, moving, each one specially formed and placed. As they plunge from the blue background over the threshold

8. www.saintjohnsbible.org.

of the horizon they come to land in the place where community is really worked out in practice. Here toes are trodden on, conflict is experienced, sadness is expressed, forgiveness is offered and received, and re-making is possible. Finally, a future dimension to community is suggested through our viewpoint from below, along with the celestial ascending arrangement of figures; we live and make in the light of the coming kingdom, aware that our making can illuminate or reveal more of God's new creation on earth. In the words of Donald Jackson: "The continuous process of remaining open and accepting of what may reveal itself through hand and heart on a crafted page is the closest I have ever come to God."[9]

## Prayer in community

Earlier we saw the importance of the natural pattern of living, praying, eating, and working together adopted by the early church. The making of signs and symbols was also key to the way they understood life in community, and, in the later medieval era art played a particular role in ways of praying in community. Wilson Yates is a pioneering writer and thinker about visual theology who states that, "The arts are important as sources for understanding the spiritual character of a particular culture."[10] The prayer books of this time reveal the importance of prayer punctuating the whole of life in the Middle Ages. For example, they offer a seamless way to pray by marking seasons, days, and hours, and giving opportunities to pause from work, to pray, to resume work, and to ultimately experience work itself as prayer, something which is at the heart of the Rule of Saint Benedict (A.D. 480). Explaining the Rule, Anselm Grün says, "He suffused the concrete aspects of life—work, prayer, community, manual labor, and art—with the spirit of the Gospel and so created a Christian way of life that still influences our Western culture."[11] Praying this way was, in fact, rooted in Jewish prayer, for example, in Psalm 119:62 the psalmist declares, "At midnight I rise to praise you." This pattern continued in early church worship practices, as the following examples make clear:

9. Ibid.
10. Vrundy and Yates, *Arts, Theology, and the Church*, 17.
11. Grün, *Benedict of Nursia*, 62.

- "One day Peter and John were going up to the temple at the hour of prayer, at three o'clock in the afternoon" (Acts 3:1).

- "About noon the next day, as they were on their journey and approaching the city, Peter went up on the roof to pray" (Acts 10:9).

- "At about midnight Paul and Silas were praying and singing hymns to God, and the prisoners were listening to them" (Acts 16:25).

Wilson Yates, again, says, "The arts provide forms integral to liturgy and worship."[12] Having understood something of the medieval mindset through prayer books, or "books of hours" is there anything for us to take away from this experience of word and picture in prayer for twenty-first-century living, where images saturate every hour of the day and night, and technology creates a very different rhythm? Discovering art forms that may lead to doxology is the subject of the making task.

## Participatory Prayer

Later in the chapter you will be invited to make a bréviary. A bréviary is a miniature form of a book of hours, a visual, devotional aid whose portable size makes it as easy as possible to use. A bréviary offers one way to be drawn into God's presence in prayer in the midst of daily life by keeping it close and allowing its physical presence, rather than the Benedictine bell, to remind you to pray at intervals.

---

12. Vrundy and Yates, *Arts, Theology, and the Church*, 17.

**Figure 38: "Travel Breviary"**

Make the bréviary according to the instructions at the end of the chapter, weaving word and image together, then try using it for a week as an aide-mémoire, mindful that you pray alone *and* with others simultaneously. As you do, reflect on your experience in the light of these words: "Living in the presence of God, according to Benedict, shapes all realms of human life: prayer, work, interaction with creation, and relationships with other people."[13] This simulation of an ancient practice is an invitation to get into someone else's shoes and to see whether that tradition can offer fresh insights. And as Donald Jackson found: "The continuous process of remaining open and accepting of what may reveal itself through hand and heart on a crafted page is the closest I have ever come to God."[14]

## Trinity shaping community: Father, Son, and Holy Spirit

Earlier in the chapter it was suggested that relationships within the Trinity provide a model for community. In this painting, *Dance of the Trinity*, 2005,[15] three individual but overlapping figures move together against a background of fragments of the sixth-century Athanasian Creed, which

13. Grün, *Benedict of Nursia*, 27.

14. http://www.saintjohnsbible.org/promotions/process/ accessed 30 May 2016.

15. gillsakakini.com.

explores the doctrine of the Trinity. The forms have a layered transparency making it unclear as to who is in front, in fact, the intention is to show each dancer taking a turn as the principal while the other two recede but are never out of contact.

**Figure 39: *Dance of the Trinity***
**by Gill C. Sakakini, 2005, ink and collage, (4' x 5')**

As the figures flow in dynamic movements they interact with and make room for each other, which reflects the mutually indwelling persons of the Trinity. As we saw in Rublev's *Icon of the Holy Trinity* the figures incline towards each other in honor, showing forth each one in turn. There is unity in diversity, "[T]he actions of each person are always co-operative . . ."[16] and this is not an exclusive dance, as shown by the invitation to either take an arm and join the dance or to step up to the waiting space at the table. This kind of welcome is enacted at a Christian art community, "The Grünewald Guild"[17] where daily rhythms include the monastic practices

---

16. Brown, *Being a Deacon Today*, 6.

17. The Grünewald Guild is in Leavenworth, WA, USA, nestled in the Cascade

of eating together, praying mattins and vespers, and tending the vegetable garden.

**Figures 40 and 41:** *Clapper-less Bells I and II*
**by Sarah Jane Gray, ceramic, 2014**

Mountains. The year-round programs draw participants from all over the world into creative exploration. www.grünewaldguild.com.

During one week community was embodied in an interactive installation, *Clapper-less Bells*, 2014, by Sarah Jane Gray,[18] which offered participants opportunities to reflect on the nature of real community. Each
one hung a ceramic bell and together they discussed parallels between the
installation and the relationships within community; how the wind affected
the bells, how the whole grew organically, how proximity changed the formation, and where beauty and disharmony, and resonance and silence were
observed. Each ceramic bell had a thread which connected it to a source
that contributed to the creative life of the whole. Let's look now at aspects
of creative life in the individual members of the Godhead.

## God the Father

The earliest expression of human community is initiated by God the Father
in Genesis 2:18 through the declaration, "It is not good that the man should
be alone; I will make him a helper as his partner." From this first blissful
community of one other person God's growing people continue to experience life together with all its high and lows. From here on in this people
work, move, and worship in families and tribes. Episodes of God's story
with his people reveal the faithful remnant embarking on travels through
feast and famine; exile and return, shared celebrations and diaspora, and as
they go they weave together myriad tales recounting shared real life during
the Old Testament pages. It is nothing if not dramatic! However, what remains consistent in the unfolding plot is the protagonist, God, who shapes,
re-shapes, and nudges on his recalcitrant people who gather in tabernacle,
temple, and synagogue. He woos them because they are made in his image
and are his "treasured possession" (Deut 7:6). Eventually he himself enters
their community as the perfect image.

In the present God's deep love for displaced people is shown through
the work of humanitarian agencies and also through engagement with the
arts. Hannah Rose Thomas[19] spends periods living and working alongside
refugees in camps in the Middle East and Europe and paints portraits that
are full of pathos and dignity. In Jordan she invited refugee children to
paint images on the stretched out canvases of old tents where she noticed a
communal theme of "home" emerging in what they produced. In their subsequent re-pitching throughout the world these "art-tents" allowed a wider

18. Photographs used by courtesy of the artist, www.sjgraystudio.com.

19. Used by courtesy of the artist, www.hannahrosethomas.com.

global community to access the crisis in a different way from that available through the media coverage. The children's experience shows that "creative activity never occurs in a vacuum, but is always connected to one's past experience, social location, and to various strands of life in the present."[20]

Figure 42: *Syrian Brother and Sister*
by Hannah Rose Thomas, oil on canvas, 2015

## God the Son

With the coming of Christ community is seen through the lens of Jesus' life, death, and resurrection and it becomes "Christian community *through* Jesus Christ and *in* Jesus Christ."[21] Although movement and pilgrimage remain themes, community is now less about the land and more about the

20. Haynes, "The Place of Art," as cited in *Arts, Theology & the Church*, 174.
21. Bonhoeffer, *Life Together*, 10. Italics mine.

kingdom of God. In the first epistle of Peter the writer captures the essence of an assembly being drawn out of former ways into something new.

> But you are a chosen race, a royal priesthood, a holy nation, God's own people, in order that you may proclaim the mighty acts of him who called you out of darkness into his marvelous light. Once you were not a people, but now you are God's people; Once you had not received mercy, but now you have received mercy. (1 Pet 2: 9–10)

The Greek word *ekklēsia*, which we translate as church and from which we derive the word ecclesiastical, underscores the sense of the people of God as those gathered and called out from former ways to new horizons.[22] The word is made up of *kaleo*, meaning "to call," and *ek*, meaning "out," and it characterizes the community as those called out to serve God. The characteristics of this organic and permeable community include a diversity of gifts, professions, nationalities, and cultures, all of which bring enormous potential to a community which is called out of darkness for a purpose. As communities work out what this looks like in practice conflict can arise and, here too, the arts can speak. Chuck Hoffmann and Peg Carlson-Hoffmann of Genesis+Art Studio[23] enable conversation where there is none through facilitating mural design and painting, and visual projects in troubled contexts, such as Northern Ireland and Palestine. They state:

> When our communities are divided over contentious issues, art can help us form questions and create opportunities for dialogue rather than verbal debate that can lead to even greater polarization. Art offers a visual language to help tell our story and birth spiritual truth. Sight can lead us to insight. Creating something together that we could not create alone is not only part of our personal creative process, we also bring this to our community art.[24]

## The Holy Spirit

Of the many roles of the Holy Spirit we focus here on revelation, particularly the way a visual encounter can change thinking. In this example it comes

22. Nouwen, *The Only Necessary Thing*, 126.

23. Peg Carlson-Hoffman + Chuck Hoffman, Genesis+Art Studio, www.genesisartstudio.com.

24. Ibid.

by way of a vision to one individual which affects an entire community. In Acts 10 the Apostle Peter sees imagery that powerfully interrupts both his noon-time prayer and his thinking.

> He saw the heaven opened and something like a large sheet coming down, being lowered to the ground by its four corners. In it were all kinds of four-footed creatures and reptiles and birds of the air. Then he heard a voice saying, "Get up, Peter; kill and eat." But Peter said, "By no means, Lord; for I have never eaten anything that is profane or unclean." The voice said to him again a second time, "What God has made clean, you must not call profane." (Acts 10:11–16)

The specific imagery that Peter sees and the words he hears are arresting. The initial impact is enduring and makes a profound impression on him: "While Peter was still thinking about the vision, the Spirit said to him . . ." (Acts 10: 19). What Peter sees in the trance significantly modifies what he had previously believed about God. His prior understanding of what was clean or unclean or who was welcome in the kingdom is re-shaped by the images before his eyes, leading him to announce boldly to the assembly in verse 28, "You yourselves know that it is unlawful for a Jew to associate with or to visit a Gentile; but God has shown me that I should not call anyone profane or unclean."

What is interesting for our exploration of creativity is the fact that Peter discovers that community in Christ includes Jews *and* Gentiles as the result of seeing an image. Creativity theorists call this "aesthetic knowledge" which is "knowing on the basis of sensible perceptions."[25] Even the art that Peter would have seen on sarcophagi showed how meaning was made by drawing on familiar symbols and filling them with fresh significance. Robin Jensen writing on this topic states that in the process of making, the arts can "promote the use of our imaginative capacities so that we can envision what we cannot actually see, taste, touch, hear and smell."[26] This is key to the way in which Christians "see" and know the three-in-one God.[27]

25. Strati, *The Aesthetic Approach in Organization Studies*, 18.

26. Eisner, *The Arts and the Creation of Minds*, 19.

27. Jensen, *The Substance of Things Seen*, 16.

Discuss

Think about the community in which you find yourself currently:

- As God calls you into an exploration of creativity, what is he calling you out from? Highlight some milestones of this journey (new discoveries, questions to ponder, insights from your project).

- Which "new land" (art-form or creative venture) are you being nudged towards?

- What does it mean to know, in Henri Nouwen's words, that God is the source of this "new life together"?

## Make

Instructions for making a bréviary

**Figure 43:**

Example

1. Punch one hole at the end of each piece of card.

2. On the first card create a monogram design for your bréviary using your initials in a horizontal or vertical direction.

3. Write the title and time of day of each office on each card beginning with Vigils (see below). Consider themes from that particular "Hour" and create thoughtful miniature designs.

4. On the reverse prayerfully select one or two verses from any of the appointed psalms for that hour.

5. Continue in the same way till you have something on each remaining card.

6. Take a piece of ribbon or cord and before you tie your cards loosely together, thread a bead onto the cord. The presence of this in your pocket invites you to stop briefly and pray the prayer at that particular time of day.

*A Selection from The Divine Office or Liturgy of the Hours*

| Name of office | Time | Readings |
|---|---|---|
| Vigils | 2:00 am | Psalm 95:1 |
| Lauds | 6:00 am | Psalm 67, 148, 149, 150 |
| Terce | 9:00 am | Psalm 119, 120, 121, 122 |
| Sext | 12 noon | Psalm 119, 123, 124, 125 |
| None | 3:00 pm | Psalm 119, 126, 127, 128 |
| Vespers | 6:00 pm | Luke 1: 46–55 (choose a portion) |
| Compline | 9:00 pm | Psalm 4, 91, 134 |

## chapter 9

# Church

For some time now there has been a turning tide of fresh openness to the arts in church, which makes these interesting and exciting times. We see churches frequently hosting art exhibitions, especially in cathedrals, and increasingly churches of all kinds and financial means are commissioning permanent and temporary pieces. Paul Bayley writes, "This changing culture has fostered a confidence in the ability of the church to move from engaging with contemporary art in an opportunist manner to thinking it central to their mission and an achievable and sustainable activity."[1]

In this chapter we envisage the church as a cairn—a pile of stones found at intervals along a trail as a memorial or way marker. How can the arts in the context of the church become a beacon that points people to God? N. T. Wright throws down the gauntlet: "Your calling may be to find new ways to tell the story of redemption, to create fresh symbols which will speak of a home for the homeless, the end of exile, the re-planting of the garden, the rebuilding of the house."[2] We look at ourselves as "living stones" gathered around the foundation stone, Christ. Here artists, writers, poets, and sculptors are fully mindful of the world's brokenness and compelled by the Christian imagination to picture the hope of a different outcome, to comment, to observe, and to announce healing, longing, and redemption.

This chapter is not the last word on the arts and the church, rather a segment of a larger conversation and a springboard. (A particularly rich resource is J. Scott Mc Elroy's *Creative Church Handbook*.) The examples

---

1. Bayley, *Contemporary Art in British Churches*, 12–13.
2. Wright, *The Challenge of Jesus*, 144.

used here are from everyday ordinary situations where congregations are imaging the story in their unique way.

## Read

> Come to him, a living stone, though rejected by mortals yet chosen and precious in God's sight, and like living stones, let yourselves be built into a spiritual house, to be a holy priesthood, to offer spiritual sacrifices acceptable to God through Jesus Christ. (1 Pet 2:4–5)

## Respond

1. Collect a handful of small stones or rocks, including one that is significantly larger. Invite the Holy Spirit to ignite your imagination. Play with the stones, engage your senses, and as you consider these verses, re-arrange the stones to express meaning. In the words of William McNamara, a Carmelite monk, *"behold"* what you have laid out, that is to say, take a "long loving look at the real."[3]

2. During Jesus' triumphal entry into Jerusalem the Pharisees asked him to silence the cries of *"Hosanna."* His reply, reported in Luke 19:39, states: "I tell you, if these were silent, the stones would shout out." Here stones are personified. What kind of words might you hear shouted out today, either within or beyond the church? Write a Haiku poem using these and your observations from question 1. The simple pattern of syllables helps to pare down our thoughts to reveal what is essential. Traditionally, haiku is written in three lines, with five syllables in the first line, seven syllables in the second, and five in the third line.

3. This question relates to the artistic project you are working on. First look at the image, *Living Stones* and read the artist's commentary.[4]

---

3. Quoted by Paintner, *The Eyes of the Heart*, 17.
4. See Appendix 5.

**Figure 44:** *Living Stones*
**by Gill C. Sakakini, textile, 2006**

To what extent is your project flowing as planned? What still remains unknown? How comfortable are you with open-ends in your work? As you discuss your reflections on this activity and the course so far, what is your experience of being built up into Christ?

## Stone: worship

As living stones we are invited to come to into the presence of *the* Living Stone, to be built up, both individually and together. The arts can help us enter the presence of God afresh in a church context by changing the space we expect to enter. During Advent one church was invited to reflect on the vertical movement towards God in worship alongside the horizontal dimension of doing so together. A star appeared to grow larger and brighter each Sunday, generating anticipation and the illusion of approaching. The star was set against layers of translucent fabric, a dark purple background, and a constellation, all of which created depth and evoked the wonder of the cosmos in relationship to humankind.

> When I look at your heavens, the work of your fingers,
>> the moon and the stars that you have established;
> what are human beings that you are mindful of them,
>> mortals that you care for them? (Ps 8:3–5)

While the congregation didn't actually move, the changing art installation helped them imagine a purposeful journey in each other's company in the same direction—expectantly, because they quickly grew to anticipate a weekly change of some kind. Tudor Powell Jones states: "curiosity is probably the most important factor in creativity[;] . . . it involves something which is partly familiar and partly unfamiliar."[5] Therefore, bringing different things together can open up space for further creative thinking about worship.

---

5. Powell, *Creative Learning in Perspective*, 11.

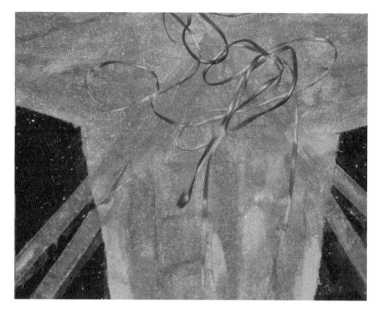

**Figures 45–48:** *Advent Series I—IV*, **textile**

## Discuss

Share any visual interpretations of the church calendar. To what extent did they facilitate worship, and why?

## Stone: difference as opportunity

Differences of opinion about art in church will certainly be held, but, navigated with sensitivity, they can be opportunities for growth. Just as the tide jostles stones against each other so can *living* stones rub each other the wrong way. Art in a church context can be a beautiful offering to God and sacrifice of praise reflecting the challenges of different people working together. The sculptures of land artists like Andy Goldsworthy consist of carefully placed rocks (imperfect in places), balancing on each other, dependent on the next for their place, each one a platform for the other, interesting in their own way, yet capable of greater beauty together. This can be a metaphor for the people of God who are carved and shaped, honed, chipped, reworked, re-arranged, and beautified by the work of the Spirit.

The church can be seen as both a crucible for discussion and refinement of thinking about the arts and a context for creativity since here living stones are re-made by the Holy Spirit through the word of God, worship, prayer, and sacraments. They move us beyond words.

## Stone: words

The arts in church are not at the expense of words, but they can help to bring balance to the Protestant (evangelical) tendency to give them priority. St. Anselm wrote of a different engagement with the word of God, one that incorporates the senses:

> Taste the goodness of your Redeemer, be on fire with love for your Saviour. Chew the honeycomb of his words, suck their flavour which is sweeter than sap, swallow their wholesome sweetness.[6]

Approaching the Bible in ways explored in this book allows us to deeply savor words by chewing over meaning, asking questions, pondering and looking. Using our senses heightens perception and is a corrective to passive reading or listening in a church context or elsewhere. Some senses are more obviously drawn on than others. For example, touching the word, as we did in the *visuo divina* exercise, poses a challenge. However, writer Stephen Pattison[7] encourages a way of seeing that seeks to reconnect touch to sight—what he calls "haptic vision"—which is cultivated by inhabiting the same space as an object and seeing and imagining texture, much as in the creative task in chapter 5. Similar to this is *Godly Play*,[8] a means of allowing children and older people or those in hospital to use objects and symbols related to the Christian story to make meaning through touch leading to wonder.

A key to mining the infinite relationships between word and image and what this might look like in the church is to establish a team. As well as church leaders, there should be representation from the curious, the practical, the visionary, and the artistically gifted. A team ensures balance and boundaries at the same time as fanning ideas into being. For example, one way to enliven biblical exegesis is to read a passage, take time to look at a

---

6. Anselm, *Prayers and Meditations*, 75.

7. Pattison, *Seeing Things*, 12.

8. www.godlyplay.uk.

painting or other artistic interpretation,[9] then return to the text to see how the imaginative encounter has permitted fresh insights. This is a form of artistic *midrash* (*mid,* meaning to seek out, *rash,* meaning to inquire) that still has deep respect for the text. Paintings should be selected wisely for this activity. Simply posting an image on a church bulletin based on the relevant Bible readings is of questionable value and can be seen as gratuitous because, while it can be argued that art speaks in and of itself, if we are to cultivate visual literacy in the church then careful guidance is needed. In the same vein, it is appropriate to encourage artists in the church to respectfully offer their own work for selection as in this way the artist is a preacher also. "There is a great need today for artists who will cultivate visionary imagination, as well as prophetic and critical faculties."[10] This is reinforced in the following extract from Pope John Paul II to all artists in 1999:

> To all who are passionately dedicated to the search for new "epiphanies" of beauty so that through their creative work as artists they may offer these as gifts to the world.
>
> "God saw all that he had made, and it was very good" (Gen 1:31) . . .
>
> None can sense more deeply than you artists, ingenious creators of beauty that you are, something of the pathos with which God at the dawn of creation looked upon the work of his hands. A glimmer of that feeling has shone so often in your eyes when—like the artists of every age—captivated by the hidden power of sounds and words, colours and shapes, you have admired the work of your inspiration, sensing in it some echo of the mystery of creation with which God, the sole creator of all things, has wished in some way to associate you.[11]

Unpacking the hidden power of words and sounds, colors and shapes is an invitation to look again at *all* the words used, whenever the church gathers. Could the church better address the wide variety of learning styles to optimize engagement? How would people encounter God differently in

---

9. The Methodist Art Collection is an excellent resource for this, http://www.methodist.org.uk/static/artcollection/index.htm.

10. Haynes, *The Place of Art,* quoted in *Arts, Theology, and the Church,* 165.

11. www.vatican.va/holy_father/john_paul_ii/letters/documents/hf_jp-ii_let_2304 1999_artists_en.html.

an occasional Eucharist whose only words were pieces of polished colored glass?

How can the arts confront the verbosity of administrative meetings and offer a means of reflection on agenda items?

For example, to engender fresh vision and purpose at the start of a new church council term, members were invited, in a prayerful context, to consider how they might approach handling the word and mission of God in that place and time in light of all who had contributed over hundreds of years.[12] Each one chose a pair of gloves to wear from a selection provided (sheepskin, latex, motorcycle, gardening, etc). As they stood side by side in a line the first person was handed a delicate, ornate, glass vase, symbolic of God's assignment. This person turned very slowly 180 degrees and carefully handed the vase to the next person who took it. Each pair of gloved hands received and passed on the vessel till it reached the end, at which point the embodied action was complete, gloves were removed, and a period of reflection followed. Participants were invited to consider how the different gloves spoke of their various gifts and approaches to handling God's task? How did the church council see the responsible role of faithfully passing on God's word to people in the present time and place? What did it mean to concentrate on receiving and passing the vase with such care? By involving each member in a creative non-threatening activity each one had an opportunity to reflect and give feedback which did not require a "right answer" but an impression through which the leading of the Holy Spirit was discerned.

## Stone: mission

In the last chapter we saw in 1 Peter 2: 9–10 that the Christian community is called *out*. The church as a royal priesthood (1 Pet 2:5) models itself on Jesus's own calling in Luke 4:18:

> The Spirit of the Lord is upon me,
>> because he has anointed me
>> to bring good news to the poor.
> He has sent me to proclaim release to the captives
>> and recovery of sight to the blind,
>> to let the oppressed go free.

12. I am grateful for partnership with Dr. Sarah Williams on this embodied action.

Being called out, is, says Peter, "*in order that you may proclaim the mighty acts of him who called you out of darkness into his marvelous light.*" As God's dearly beloved people it is essential to remember "the God of *mission* has a *church* not that the *church* of God has a *mission.*"[13] This is not all about the church, this is the *missio dei*, (mission of God) and it is God who invites the church to discover what it looks like to be *sent* into the world, as we saw in chapter 3. The church, Christ's hands and feet in the world, is variously gifted and as it continues to understand itself in light of the life, death, resurrection, and ascension of Jesus Christ it is equipped and poised to act creatively and responsively, quick on the heels of where and how God is working. As we have seen, living stones are capable of re-making and re-creating at the impulse of the Holy Spirit, a dynamism which is captured by the poet-priest R. S. Thomas in his description of God's activity—he is "such a fast God, always before us, and leaving as we arrive."[14] As the church keeps pace with the activity of God it is fresh, alert, ready to step into the dance of the Trinity—ever energetic, ever innovative, ever outward looking. So how can this be done?

In spite of the enormous diversity in the gathered church it *is* possible to settle on an "arrangement of stones" which suits a church's particular shape. Consider the following for your particular context:

## Practical pointers

### Know your environment

Think of your locality first of all. In some church traditions the role of a deacon is to "understand the territory, to be wise in the ways of the world . . . to search out and reach into forgotten corners . . . ." They are to be "the eyes and ears of the church in the locality, immersed deeply in life and able to understand what is going on."[15] However, it is for *everyone* to notice how communities change, to see who comes and goes, to seek gaps where the church could artfully connect with certain groups, or offer a service.

Next, remember the value placed on innovation in western culture and that most communication takes place through the transmission of fast-paced images. "The message of the gospel is timeless, but Jesus, Paul and

13. Pritchard, *The Life and Work, of a Priest*, 117.

14. Davis, *Poetry: R. S. Thomas*, 97.

15. Brown, *Being a Deacon Today*, 60–61.

the prophets regularly spoke in the vernacular of their culture. . . . This doesn't have to be some desperate attempt to be 'relevant.' God's love is always relevant. But our culture's language is art and creativity."[16]

## Pay attention at boundary places

How is your church communicating welcome at the physical boundaries? How might the arts help people cross the thresholds between church and other places such as school, sports facilities, cultural centres, businesses, and shopping centres? "These thresholds are important, they remind us where we are and what sort of people we are called to be. As you cross them, be attentive to their meaning."[17]

## Create rituals

The word ritual may have a negative connotation for some as it can sound dry and prescriptive when used of church. However, in light of the following description we discover that rituals go beyond church and are constantly being created, revealing a need to give expression to a feeling, concern, or proclamation. Sociologist, Linda Woodhead[18] offers some characteristics of ritual:

1. Ritual is a cocoon. It involves a boundaried space (church, a cast circle, etc.) and time (it has a clear beginning and end). In a cocoon, something transformative happens and so it is with ritual—those taking part move from one state to another.

2. Ritual involves the body and "things." Though there have been many attempts at "virtual" rituals, it seems that being physically present is crucial. "Things" can be used as props or created or destroyed during ritual. But they're almost always there.

16. McElroy, *Creative Church Handbook*, 23.

17. Brown, Sermon: *Thresholds, Boundaries, and Barriers*. 24 April 2016. https://www.durhamcathedral.co.uk/worshipandmusic/sermon-archive/thresholds-boundaries-and-barriers.

18. Woodhead, Extract from the transcript from The Art of Ritual Conference, Brighton. 5 December 2016. http://artofritual.weebly.com/conference-schedule.html.

3. Ritual focuses. It is a focusing lens which makes things special, singles out, stabilizes and dignifies. (For example, at a wedding two people are magnified and honored.)

4. Ritual connects. It makes participants part of a bigger picture—social, natural, historical, and spiritual. It can make the private public or the public private.

### Re-ritualization and forging new patterns

> Ritual is changing from obligation to voice and choice . . . we have gone from ritual regulation (the prescribed services in churches, etc.) to de-regulation (this started at events such as [Princess] Diana's death—no one waited for traditional ritual-makers but created their own). Now there is a sort of "re-ritualisation"—an explosion of creativity and experiment by artists, celebrants, priests, theatre and the like.[19]

Many of these aspects featured in an installation, "Prayer Wall," which offered opportunities for contemplative personal prayer in a "cocoon" space. This was a large, well-lit atrium entrance to a college with a cafe and abundant seating providing a habitual meeting place for students and public alike. At the end of a defined period of time the art was destroyed. A mural-sized painting was cut into hundreds of small squares with numbers on the reverse, corresponding to an identically numbered grid on a prominent wall. The colorful pieces were placed in baskets around the area with clear written instructions for selecting a square, reflecting on its colors and shapes, and writing a prayer on the reverse, finally sticking it on the corresponding square. This was an embodied action, as in order for the piece to remain securely in place it needed to be pressed down for several minutes, causing a person to linger. Over several weeks this image, known only to its creators, gradually took form and provoked conversation and a sense of belonging and ownership in the process.

19. Ibid.

Figure 49: "Basket of pieces"

Figure 50: *Prayer Wall*, detail, 2007 (6' x 4')

To be church in this flowing relational manner is part of what it means to be human and therefore, as we act creatively in the world and beyond, and as we foster creativity in congregations and beyond, we encourage people to grow into who they were created to be.

## Stone: participation

> There is no other place in our culture except the church, where we go expecting to simply get a unilateral form of communication, i.e., someone behind a box speaking, and an audience out there receiving. Go into a school, college or university, and you expect multimedia; go to the mall and you expect visual displays, go downtown to the city center and you expect to see artwork, sidewalk performers and the like. Only at church is it common—and too often accepted—that the medium will be simply the spoken word with little or no interaction or participation.[20]

When participation occurs it cuts across any isolationist or passive tendencies and it means, in John Pritchard's words, "the cauldron is bubbling and not stagnant."[21] Stagnancy sets in when spectators watch performers, but wider involvement gives rise to playful experimentation, trial and error, surprise, and re-negotiation as a satisfactory outcome is worked out. What is gained along the way is as significant as the end result and encapsulates what it means to function interdependently as the people of God, serving others and valuing their contributions. Engaging in this way includes a greater number of people and honors the contribution of each one. Leadership, however, needs to be serving, strong, collaborative, and not too risk-averse. Remember God giving Adam free rein to name the animals?

## Stone: play

One of the bi-products of participation can be play. This is something we rarely associate with church but William Dyrness suggests, "one of the critical functions art may perform is to bring the notion of play back into the center of our lives where it belongs."[22] The Bible speaks of delighting in the

20. *Preaching and the Arts*, www.homileticsonline.com.
21. Pritchard, *The Life and Work of a Priest*, 134.
22. Dyrness, *Visual Faith*, 140.

Lord, glorifying him and enjoying him forever, especially in some psalms; David played, danced, and leapt before the Lord, and Psalm 148 in particular paints a spirited picture of hail, snow, sea monsters, and creeping things, all giving God glory. "Authentic play is a gift from a generous and creative God which is characterised by freedom and relationship."[23] How do we recover a sense of playful participation in which *everyone* can have a role?

Nowhere do we see this more clearly than in God's plans for participation in the details of the tabernacle. Aesthetics are important enough that the Holy Spirit gifts and designates Bezalel and Oholiab for the task of designing the worship space and charges them with taking up raw materials of creation to make a sacred space and objects which point worshippers to God.

> The LORD spoke to Moses: See, I have called by name Bezalel son of Uri son of Hur, of the tribe of Judah: and I have filled him with divine spirit, with ability, intelligence, and knowledge in every kind of craft, to devise artistic designs, to work in gold, silver, and bronze, in cutting stones for setting, and in carving wood, in every kind of craft. Moreover, I have appointed with him Oholiab son of Ahisamach, of the tribe of Dan; and I have given skill to all the skillful, so that they may make all that I have commanded you: the tent of meeting, and the ark of the covenant, and the mercy seat that is on it, and all the furnishings of the tent, the table and its utensils, and the pure lampstand with all its utensils, and the altar of incense, and the altar of burnt offering with all its utensils, and the basin with its stand, and the finely worked vestments, the holy vestments for the priest Aaron and the vestments of his sons, for their service as priests, and the anointing oil and the fragrant incense for the holy place. They shall do just as I have commanded you. (Exod 31:1–11)

But this is not just for the recognized artists. Imagine Moses, having just received God's meticulous instructions, now attempts to persuade the Israelites that they each have something worthwhile to contribute to the elaborate construction! In spite of the almost certain cries of "but I'm not creative" and "what about the cost?" Moses evidently mobilizes the people to create a dwelling place of immense beauty befitting the powerful, faithful, and creative God. We note that *everyone* participates in the artistic venture—it is not for perceived creatives or for those who choose this activity over another. God invites *all* the Israelites, via Moses, to offer something in

---

23. Ong in preface to "Man at Play," xiii.

the way of materials in a very accessible manner. The list in Exodus 25:3–7 comprises precious as well as expensive items ("gold, silver, and bronze") and also readily available ones ("goats' hair, tanned rams' skins, fine leather, acacia wood"). The people have a fundamental role to play by sourcing the materials and fulfilling the confident expectation God has in Moses: ". . . so you shall make it" (Exod 25:9). It is interesting here to notice God's instructions include the making of images, cherubim, almond flowers, and pomegranates, which represent heavenly creatures and the fruitful bounty of the earth. It's wise to remember in our own making that an image is different from an idol, i.e., from "something which would be worshipped as a symbol of allegiance to anything or anyone other than the One Almighty God."[24]

## Re-enacting the tabernacle in play-ful contemporary worship

A congregation entered into the story in the following engaging way. Two weeks before the event large rolls of paper like scrolls were hung in an obvious place on which were listed every item needed for the tabernacle, down to simple rolls of tape and adapted recipes for Middle Eastern cookies. Families and individuals signed up to supply items.

On the day the tabernacle, outer courts, and holy of holies were constructed in the main worship space with poles and fabrics. In other spaces some baked flatbreads, others, including children, arranged themselves around a piece of cloth intended for the table of presence, which had already been hand-dyed by a fabric artist, and they helped print stylized fruits. Liturgy was written for the service by one group; another arranged candles for the lampstand and prepared bowls for water and incense. Everyone had a role to play.

On hearing a child's solo voice moving among them singing a song about the holy of holies all were to gather in the outer courts. In a graceful procession everything was brought into the tabernacle followed by the entire congregation who heard the tear of a curtain and walked through it, transitioning to New Testament times. Through this multi-sensory experience they grasped something physical about the free access to God afforded them through Jesus's death on the cross and resurrection. In this place, huddled together as the body of Christ, the Eucharist was celebrated.

---

24. Brand and Chaplin, *Art & Soul*, 79.

## Make

- Design a project for the exhibition which either explores the theme of church, or which can inhabit a place of worship.
- Think about how you can collaborate with others.
- Factor in any practical requirements for the exhibition.
- You may wish to draw on the following examples as a springboard for your project.

## Example 1

The goal of an installation called *Threaded Lives* was to enable a congregation to know each other better by associating faces with names. Rather than simply labelling photos on a notice board (which would have ticked the box), a woven artwork grew out of theological reflection on what it actually means to be alongside each other as the body of Christ (living stones) in a particular place.

- We are made in the image of God (represented by the photo each person provided, which was then laminated).
- We bear the effects of sin and brokenness (symbolized by cutting the photo into horizontal strips).
- We are redeemed by Christ's death and the assurance of new life through the resurrection (symbolized by weaving the pieces back together).

This new image was built up by members of the congregation weaving the images together through the warp threads over a period of time. As each face was re-made, the individual portraits became greater than the sum of their parts. In addition to its practical function the installation invited deeper reflection on how each member (living stone) is valued; what it means to be woven in alongside others of different ages and personalities, and how a church makes room at the permeable edges to thread others in.

**Figure 51: Setting up the warp**     **Figure 52: Weaving in process**

## Example 2

Consider the ways in which the following piece shows the whole and the parts simultaneously.[25] What effect does this have on how we see the image? How might this approach be a tool for thinking about living stones?

25. Used by courtesy of the artist.

**Figure 53:** *Inside my Head*
**by Maddy Weavers, 2016 (2' x 1.5')**

chapter 10

# Consummation

## "And I turned to see the voice"

It is perhaps no surprise that John's apocalyptic vision in the book of Revelation is the most widely illustrated biblical book in Western European art. Nicknamed "John the seer" due to his highly visual language, his book contains over sixty references to "seeing."[1]

Here, word and image, hearing and seeing, work dynamically together: John turns to "see the voice" (Rev 1:12). Yet biblical exegesis has often focused on the *textual* interpretation of these visions at the expense of the *visual*.[2] Perhaps this imbalance arises from a wariness of taking the images too literally—or from a wariness of the imagination itself. Yet the book of Revelation is image-rich. The images move fluidly: sometimes they morph, sometimes they collide, always they require the imagination to host them generously.

### The eagle's view

As we saw at the start of this course, John is often represented by an eagle in church tradition.[3] This is based partly on the description of the fourth

1. O'Hear, *Contrasting Images of the Book of Revelation in Late Medieval and Early Modern Art*, 1. O'Hear also highlights how often the word "like" is used to introduce imagery in the book.

2. Ibid.

3. For an example, see the silhouetted illumination of an eagle in the Gospel of John

living creature in Revelation 4:7, but also on John's tendency to soar high. Now, exiled on the island of Patmos, it is as if John is picked up in eagle's talons and can see far. Rather than resigning himself to the present and allowing that present to shape the future, he is captured by a vision of what God can and surely will do in the future, and this vision transforms his present landscape.[4]

From this eagle's view we see the book of Revelation as the tale of two cities.[5] There is Rome, described in Revelation 17:1 as the "great whore,"[6] and there is the New Jerusalem. Rome was an ever-present reality and must have seemed an invincible power to the beleaguered Christians facing persecution. These men and women would have needed to see that promised New Jerusalem. From the eagle's perspective, John *sees the voice* that speaks the last word on human history—"It is done!" (Rev 21:6).[7] Finally, in the new reign, God gets to have his way, "on earth as it is in heaven." In this theonomy (God's rule), *shalom* is restored.

## Tragedy or comedy?

However, as we follow the contours of the salvation story to its dramatic conclusion, one truth emerges: things will get worse before they get better. This book plays out the story of sin and redemption on a grand scale. Satan, bounced out of heaven through the death and resurrection of Jesus Christ, is "filled with fury because he knows his time is short" (Rev 12:12)—and he is lashing out. At times, it seems that all hell is being unleashed and the salvation plot is unraveling.

The extract below is from W.B. Yeats' poem, "The Second Coming." Written in 1919, it evokes a sense of global unraveling. The anticipation of impending apocalypse is palpable. Millions had been killed in World War I; survivors were being wiped out by a flu epidemic; revolution was erupting in Russia; and Ireland, Yeats' home country, was experiencing the Easter

---

in the St. John's Bible (http://www.saintjohnsbible.org).

4. Jeremy Begbie explores this well in "The Future: Looking to the Future: A Hopeful Subversion," in Taylor (ed.), *For the Beauty of the Church*, 167.

5. Greenslade, *The Big Story*, 805.

6. With biblical echoes of Babylon.

7. Greenslade, *The Big Story*, 811.

Rising and massacre.[8] Yeats employs the image of a trained falcon and its master:

> Turning and turning in the widening gyre
> The falcon cannot hear the falconer;
> Things fall apart; the centre cannot hold;
> Mere anarchy is loosed upon the world . . . .[9]

## Reflect

- Read the extract above. How do the images of falcon/falconer work on you?

- In what way do "things fall apart" globally today? How does the falconer's voice seem to be lost?

- What image would you choose today to evoke a world spiraling out of control?

The word "apocalypse" refers to an "unveiling," and in John's seventh and final vision, the veil is lifted on the ending of this story. Into this world of rebellion, God speaks clearly and powerfully, giving John a vision that breathes hope into weary faith and trains our eyes on the big story.

At times, it has been hard to tell whether this story is a comedy or tragedy. The ending of a drama is usually the deciding factor. A traditional tragedy, no matter how comic along the way, will always end in the death of the main character; a comedy, however, ends in a wedding and often a feast. Ultimately, the salvation story, no matter how tragic some of its acts, will end as a *comedy*. There will be both a wedding and a feast! Satan will not have the last laugh. In the final chapters of Revelation you sense that all of heaven has been holding its breath for this final consummation:

> Let us rejoice and be glad
> and give him the glory!
> For the wedding of the Lamb has come,
> and his bride has made herself ready.
> (Rev 19:7)

---

8. Morley, *Haphazard by Starlight*, 46.
9. Yeats, "The Second Coming," as cited in Morley, *Haphazard by Starlight*, 45.

# Read

So let's turn to this dazzling, hope-restoring vision now. Read the text below slowly. Allow your imagination to "see the voice."

## NEW CREATION

Then I saw a new heaven and a new earth; for the first heaven and the first earth had passed away, and the sea was no more. And I saw the holy city, the new Jerusalem, coming down out of heaven from God, prepared as a bride adorned for her husband. And I heard a loud voice from the throne saying,

"See, the home of God is among mortals.
He will dwell with them;
　　they will be his peoples,
　　and God himself will be with them;
　　he will wipe every tear from their eyes.
Death will be no more;
　　mourning and crying and pain will be no more,
　　for the first things have passed away."

And the one who was seated on the throne said, "See, I am making all things new." Also he said, "Write this, for these words are trustworthy and true." Then he said to me, "It is done! I am the Alpha and the Omega, the beginning and the end. To the thirsty I will give water as a gift from the spring of the water of life. Those who conquer will inherit these things, and I will be their God and they will be my children. But as for the cowardly, the faithless, the polluted, the murderers, the fornicators, the sorcerers, the idolaters, and all liars, their place will be in the lake that burns with fire and sulfur, which is the second death."

## NEW JERUSALEM

Then one of the seven angels who had the seven bowls full of the seven last plagues came and said to me, "Come, I will show you the bride, the wife of the Lamb." And in the spirit he carried me away to a great, high mountain and showed me the holy city Jerusalem coming down out of heaven from God. It has the glory of God and a radiance like a very rare jewel, like jasper, clear as crystal. It has a great, high wall with twelve gates, and at the gates twelve angels, and on the gates are inscribed the names of the twelve tribes of the Israelites; on the east three gates, on the north three gates, on the south three gates, and on the west three gates. And the wall of the city has twelve foundations, and on them are the twelve names of the twelve apostles of the Lamb.

The angel who talked to me had a measuring rod of gold to measure the city and its gates and walls. The city lies foursquare, its length the same as its width; and he measured the city with his rod, fifteen hundred miles; its length and width and height are equal. He also measured its wall, one hundred forty-four cubits by human measurement, which the angel was using. The wall is built of jasper, while the city is pure gold, clear as glass. The foundations of the wall of the city are adorned with every jewel; the first was jasper, the second sapphire, the third agate, the fourth emerald, the fifth onyx, the sixth carnelian, the seventh chrysolite, the eighth beryl, the ninth topaz, the tenth chryso-prase, the eleventh jacinth, the twelfth amethyst. And the twelve gates are twelve pearls, each of the gates is a single pearl, and the street of the city is pure gold, transparent as glass.

I saw no temple in the city, for its temple is the Lord God the Almighty and the Lamb. And the city has no need of sun or moon to shine on it, for the glory of God is its light, and its lamp is the Lamb. The nations will walk by its light, and the kings of the earth will bring their glory into it. Its gates will never be shut by day—and there will be no night there. People will bring into it the glory and the honor of the nations. But nothing unclean will enter it, nor anyone who practices abomination or falsehood, but only those who are written in the Lamb's book of life.

## RIVER OF LIFE

Then the angel showed me the river of the water of life, bright as crystal, flowing from the throne of God and of the Lamb through the middle of the street of the city. On either side of the river is the tree of life with its twelve kinds of fruit, producing its fruit each month; and the leaves of the tree are for the healing of the nations. Nothing accursed will be found there any more. But the throne of God and of the Lamb will be in it, and his servants will worship him; they will see his face, and his name will be on their foreheads. And there will be no more night; they need no light of lamp or sun, for the Lord God will be their light, and they will reign forever and ever.

And he said to me, "These words are trustworthy and true, for the Lord, the God of the spirits of the prophets, has sent his angel to show his servants what must soon take place."

"See, I am coming soon! Blessed is the one who keeps the words of the prophecy of this book." (Rev 21:1—22:7)

## Respond

You might like to annotate the margins in the text above with words or sketches in response to these questions:

- In this vision of the New Jerusalem what do you notice is there? Allow these images to reverberate in your imagination as you write or draw in the margins.

- What visual threads from the salvation story are brought to fulfillment in this passage?[10]

- What is different about the New Jerusalem? What is missing? Make a list of those people who will be out of a job there!

## A garden-city

This city is a garden-city,[11] a vision that consummates various elements of the garden of Eden, such as the river of life (Rev 22:1), and the tree of life (Rev 22:2). This consummation of the salvation story was only made possible through Jesus' death on the cross. In Roger Wagner's stained glass window below, we see what the cross has secured for us, in the form of a flourishing tree of life. Its branches are full of blossom, and from its roots pours the river of life.

10. You might like to consider the garden, the precious stones, Jerusalem, the wedding, the river, the tree, light, etc.

11. Greenslade, *The Big Story*, 808.

**Figure 54: *The Flowering Tree***
**by Roger Wagner, St. Mary the Virgin church, Iffley**

Reflect

- Spend some time looking at the stained glass image. What is your eye drawn to?
- How does the image converse with the Revelation passage above?
- Voice your thanks for what Christ is bringing to flourish in your own creativity.

Some confess to a dread that heaven will be dull. They fear that there will be endless time and nothing to do with it. Many people speak about it as if it were devoid of "stuff;" or as if we will all be floating around in a mystical vapor. Yet, as Greenslade points, out John's vision shows that God has not "written off" his good creation. Greenslade argues that our future environment is not heaven "in some ethereal, other-worldly sense, but rather a redeemed earth."[12] Heaven will therefore be anything but dull.

In the New Jerusalem there will be creatureliness, materiality—lots of it—of all different colors and textures with which to make and tend. There will also be face-to-face seeing with God, just as it was in the garden before Adam and Eve's expulsion. Jesus' return will bring an end to separation anxiety.

Just as the *shalom* between humankind and God is restored, so too is it restored between people. Notice that the New Jerusalem is an *international* city, with multitudes thronging from every tribe, people, and language group. This is a celebration of unity-within-difference. The city is made up of twelve tribes (named on the gates) and twelve apostles (named in the foundation stones). The number twelve reminds us that the family, promised long ago to Abraham, is finally complete.

## The New Jerusalem

One significant characteristic of the New Jerusalem is its shape. Measuring 12,000 stadia high, long, and wide it is a perfect cube, like the most holy place in the temple (1 Kgs 6:20).[13] The temple was the place that every Jewish pilgrim ached to be near (Ps 84) because there, in the holy of holies, God's presence was believed to dwell in concentrated form. However, now, in the New Jerusalem, *everywhere* is filled with God's presence.[14] It is achingly glorious, as the following artwork suggests.

*De/coding the Apocalypse*[15] is a digital media exhibition by artist Michael Takeo Magruder that takes a contemporary and evocative look at the book of Revelation through a series of digital visions. One installation contains QR codes that can be scanned with smart phones to view content; another, entitled *Playing the Apocalypse*, uses graphic videogame scenes playing on a triptych of screens that are reminiscent of John Martin's nineteenth-century apocalyptic landscapes. A third installation comprises

12. Ibid., 800.

13. Greenslade, *The Big Story*, 805.

14. Ibid.

15. Visit http://www.takeo.org/nspace/2014-decoding-the-apocalypse/ to view documentation of the exhibition *De/coding the Apocalypse* by Michael Takeo Magruder.

a large floating projection and a single Oculus Rift headset, inviting us to interpret John's image of the heavenly city into a four dimensional virtual space. Entitled *A New Jerusalem*, this artwork is algorithmically generated using the encoded text of Revelation's description of the prophesied city, blended with Google Maps' data of present-day Jerusalem. This installation points to a city made gloriously new.

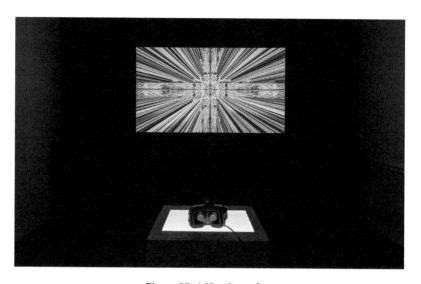

Figure 55: *A New Jerusalem*
by Michael Takeo Magruder, 2014, virtual reality installation[16]

16. Installation as part of *De/coding the Apocalypse*, solo exhibition, Somerset House, London, UK, 2014. Photograph by Jana Chiellino. Courtesy of the artist.

**Figure 56:** *A New Jerusalem*
**by Michael Takeo Magruder, 2014, virtual reality installation.**
**Still image of an internal view of the city**[17]

## Reflect

Take some time to look at *A New Jerusalem*. We suggest you go to http://www.takeo.org/nspace/2014-dta-new-jerusalem/ to see more images of the city.

1. What impact do the different perspectives bring to your perception of the New Jerusalem?

2. Pay attention to the shape and color of the city. How does the light work on you? What does it evoke?

3. What does the space open up in your own imagination? How does it enrich your perception of Revelation 21?

4. In putting on the headset, we enter a four dimensional space. How might you create your own piece of art that helps people enter into John's vision of the New Jerusalem?

17. Courtesy of the artist.

## Coming Home

In one sense, this image of the New Jerusalem is not a new image; it was given long ago to the Old Testament prophets, most particularly to Ezekiel (Ezek 28:12–16).[18] The city points back. Some have even called what we see in Revelation 21–22 "the new genesis." Perhaps, as T. S. Eliot suggests,

> The end of all our exploring
>
> Will be to arrive where we started
>
> And know the place for the first time.[19]

This will be a homecoming like no other. As the Unicorn cries at the end of *The Last Battle,* "I have come home at last! This is my real country! I belong here. This is the land I have been looking for all my life, though I never knew it till now. . . . Come further up, come further in!"[20]

Look at the painting below.

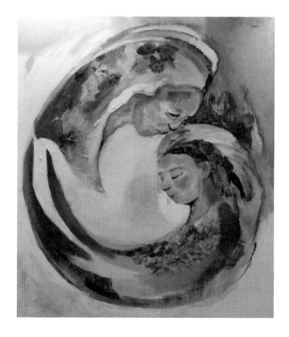

**Figure 57: *Coming Home***
**by Ros Mansfield, 2014, Guildford Baptist Church**[21]

18. Greenslade, *The Big Story,* 803.

19. Eliot, "Little Gidding," *The Four Quartets.*

20. Lewis, *The Last Battle,* 758.

21. Courtesy of the artist. For more information about this painting, see Appendix

## Reflect

- In the painting a mother holds her child. How does the shape of these figures contribute to a sense of "coming home" for you?

- What does their embrace speak to you of? Does it point back to other parts of the salvation story?

- This is a mixed-media work. How do the different textures invite you to "come further up, come further in"?

## Make

Greenslade writes, "in the new Jerusalem, every human potential will be realized, all seeds will bear fruit, all history and culture will be redeemed and made good to the glory of the Creator."[22]

1. In what way will the fulfillment of John's vision in Revelation 21–22 be a "homecoming" for you and for this world?

2. How would you picture this homecoming? You could choose to do this personally (for yourself or someone else) or for the wider world.

3. How might you express it in a creative medium, either visually or through words?[23]

Take a first draft or some ideas along to your final session.

## Hope-ful waiting

It is often said that, living between Christ's resurrection and final return, we are "living between the now and the not-yet." What is spoken of less frequently, however, is *how* to live at this threshold of hope. Waiting can become a mere endurance test and, as the writer of Proverbs states, "Where there is no vision, the people perish" (Prov 29:18). John's visions give hope to Christians struggling under the iron power of Rome; he helps them see

5. For information about the artist and her work, visit http://www/soulspacepilgrimage.co.uk.

22. Greenslade, *The Big Story*, 807.

23. We appreciate that you may be working on an exhibition piece at this stage so may not have much time to develop this task. However, you might like to use this piece for the exhibition or to give it to someone as a gift.

in a kaleidoscopic blaze of color that God's reality is more gloriously *real* than that of Rome.

Re-visioning by the Spirit helps us to wait, not with the joyless stoicism that the church in Ephesus fell into (Rev 2), but with what Begbie calls "hopeful subversion."[24] We allow the future to act back on the present. As Quash writes, "Our imagination of future consummation is resourced in such a way that we live differently *now*. Given a taste for that consummation . . . our principle task is 'not to fall backwards' (Rom 8:15)."[25] Imaginative making plays a significant role in this waiting. By unveiling the unseen world, John commits a prophetic act of hope. As makers with baptized imaginations,[26] we can do the same.

## Whose imagination will we dwell in?

The book of Revelation raises the all-important question: whose imagination will we dwell in while we wait? The prophetic imagination is key to helping us abide in God's own imagination.[27]

Brueggemann cites Lawrence Thornton's novel, *Imagining Argentina*, which evokes the power of the imagination to bring change to those living under the iron regime of General Guzman's military dictatorship. The protagonist, Carlos Rueda, has the gift of "sign acts" to effect change, much as the biblical prophets' sign acts bring God's judgment into effect.[28] Carlos's contemporaries are driven by skepticism, convinced that tanks cannot be confronted by stories, nor helicopters by "mere imagination." In his commentary on the novel, however, William Cavanaugh, notices that:

> Carlos, on the other hand, rightly grasps that the contest is not between imagination and the real, but between two types of imagination, that of the generals and that of their opponents. The nightmare world of torture and disappearance of bodies is inseparable from the generals' imagination of what Argentina and Argentinians are. Carlos realizes that "he was being dreamed by

24. Ibid.

25. Quash, *Found Theology*, 279.

26. "Baptised imagination" is a term borrowed from C. S. Lewis in *Surprised by Joy*, 146.

27. Brueggemann, Preface to *The Prophetic Imagination*, xx.

28. E.g. the linen loincloth and the wine-jars (Jer 13).

(General) Guzman and the others, that he had been living inside their imagination."[29]

The book of Revelation was given to a beleaguered church to unveil a more authentic, robust reality than that of Rome's. It brings news that God's kingdom is closer than we think. The arts can help to radically re-vision the world in the light of this hope. They are not merely there as "eye candy" to spruce up a church building; they are there to image the story. As Tom Wright states:

> We have lived for too long with the arts as the pretty bit around the edge with the reality as a non-artistic thing in the middle...And if you want to find sentimental art then, tragically, the church is often a good place to look, as people when they want to paint religious pictures screen out the nasty bits. But genuine art, I believe, takes seriously the fact that the world is full of the glory of God, and that it will be full as the waters cover the sea, and, at present (Rom 8), it is groaning in travail. Genuine art responds to that triple awareness: of what is true (the beauty that is there), of what will be true (the ultimate beauty), and of the pain of the present, and holds them together as the psalms do, and asks why and what and where are we. You can do that in music, and you can do that in painting. And our generation needs us to do that not simply to decorate the gospel but to announce the gospel. Because again and again, when you can do that you open up hermeneutic space for people whose minds are so closed by secularism that they just literally cannot imagine any other way of the world being. I have debated...with colleagues in the New Testament guild who refuse to believe in the bodily resurrection and, again and again, the bottom line is when they say 'I just can't imagine that', the answer is, 'Smarten up your imagination.' And the way to do that is not to beat them over the head with dogma but to create a world of mystery and beauty and possibility, that actually there are some pieces of music which when you come out of them it is much easier to say, 'I believe in the Father and the Son and the Holy Spirit' than when you went in.[30]

This is a good quotation to finish the course with. Today, we want to use our imaginations to announce the gospel and give vision to this promised world, just as John did.

29. Thornton, as cited in Cavanaugh, *Torture and Eucharist*, 279.

30. Wright, "Jesus, the Cross and the Power of God." Conference paper presented at European Leaders' Conference.

One day the waiting will come to an end. Phillip Yancey tells the story of a German prison camp in which some Americans secretly built a radio. As a result, they were one of the first to hear the news that the German High Command had surrendered, thus ending the war. Due to a communication fault, this news had not yet reached the German guards. Not surprisingly, it spread fast through the prisoners and a loud celebration broke out. Yancey writes:

> For three days the prisoners were hardly recognizable. They sang, waved at guards, laughed at the German shepherd dogs, and shared jokes over meals. On the fourth day, they awoke to find that all Germans had fled, leaving the gates unlocked. The time of waiting had come to an end.[31]

We know how this story will end, and knowing makes all the difference. May the things we make, in our different callings and with our different creative media, voice prophetic hope until that day when Christ returns.

31. Yancey, "Believing in Advance," 221.

# Appendix 1

## Visuo divina

Although *lectio divina,* divine reading, is widely practiced as a way of moving through a text attentively and meditatively, *visuo* divina (a visual version of it) helps us open up the word with images. Both approaches permit ways of lingering with just one word or short phrase, but *visuo divina* helps us to see the word in a different way too

## Materials on each table

- Several "Brusho" inks (water-based colored inks), made by ColourCraft and used by diluting powder with water in pots. (Watercolor paints or acrylics work, but lack the vibrancy and versatility of inks).
- A selection of Brusho pots, opened.
- Protective gloves
- Pots of water
- 5 cm, or 2 inch wide sponge brushes
- Sheet of heavy (120 lb) white paper (size A3, or 11 x 17 inches tabloid/ledger)
- Piece of white candle per person
- Two oil pastels or wax crayons per person
- Any additional pens people wish to have

## Passage

> In the day that the Lord God made the earth and the heavens, when no plant of the field was yet in the earth and no herb of the

field had yet sprung up—for the Lord God had not caused it to rain upon the earth, and there was no one to till the ground, but a stream would rise from the earth, and water the whole face of the ground—then the Lord formed man from the dust of the ground, and breathed into his nostrils the breath of life; and the man became a living thing. And the Lord God planted a garden in Eden, in the east; and there he put the man whom he had formed. Out of the ground the Lord God made to grow every tree that is pleasant to the sight and good for food. (Gen 2: 4–9)

## *Lectio:* reading and listening

(If doing this in a group arrange in advance for four people to read the passage aloud, at a slower pace than usual. In a group setting a leader would read the instructions aloud.)

1. Read aloud the passage or hear it read. Listen for a phrase or particular word that strikes you. Stay with that phrase and repeat it in your mind.

2. When the reading is over, pause. Consciously relax your shoulders and loosen your arms.

3. Pick up the piece of wax and in the center of your large paper write your word or phrase. Use your whole arm either in free-flowing script, or print, but *press down* very firmly.

4. Be aware of the word transitioning from your mind, through your physical body, to the paper.

5. Close your eyes. With your fingertips try to trace the forms you have made. *Feel* the word.

## *Meditatio:* reflecting on the word

1. As you listen for a second time, let God's love deeply penetrate your being. Allow the word to work within you and travel with your thoughts.

2. Read the passage.

3. Take two pastels or crayons and hold them in your hand. Reflect on their materiality, their "this-ness." Hold them together as you would a

pencil. Re-write your word/phrase firmly in double style many times emanating out in different directions from the original wax.

4. Bring your experience, thoughts, feelings, hopes, desires, and intuition to join the word. How do you experience the word now?

## *Oratio:* the word touches the heart

1. As you listen a third time, encourage your heart to remain attentive. Invite the Holy Spirit to wash over you and respond in prayer flowing out of meditation.

2. Read the passage.

3. Take a wide sponge brush and load it with ink or paint. Draw it freely across the central wax word or phrase.

4. Soak a fresh, smaller sponge brush in water and paint a few strokes, or make droplets elsewhere. Carefully sprinkle a *few* granules of Brusho powder onto the wet areas (with gloved hand, as Brusho stains temporarily). Add other colors in ink, tilt the paper gently so the inks spread beyond the words.

5. Carefully turn the paper around to see if anything strikes you differently. Make any marks or symbols, or write words to express your thoughts.

6. Be aware of what is rising within you and how the word is touching you. Talk to God about it silently.

## *Contemplatio:* contemplation: entering the silence

1. Read the passage for the final time in silence yourself.

2. Experience a loving, peaceful inflow of God and a sense of divine calm.

3. Allow yourself to move beyond thoughts and images. Simply *be* in God's presence.

# Appendix 2: The Project

During the course you will have the opportunity to create a piece of visual art or writing that gives voice to some aspect of the salvation story, as outlined in these chapters. It could be a poem, painting, textile, photograph (or series of photographs), film, or dance piece. What you make will then contribute to an *Imaging the Story* exhibition that will be held in the local community, at a church, café, or other community place.

These are the steps you'll need to take to prepare for the project:

1. Identify a particular chapter in the book that you'd like to respond to creatively. (See ideas below.) If you're interested in a chapter that your group has not yet covered, feel free to read on by yourself.

2. Read the biblical passage from that chapter and allow your imagination to roam the text. Are there any particular words or images that the Holy Spirit highlights for you? Look back at the themes from that chapter. What particularly caught your imagination here?

3. Draft some ideas and run them by your group. Factor in any practical requirements for the exhibition. Tweak where necessary.

4. Get making your piece!

5. Mary's song picks up on other songs in the Bible. (See chapter 4— Conception.) Consider how your ideas weave into the salvation story and how they intersect with it. When you exhibit, show how your piece has responded to the biblical text and is imaging the story.

## Project ideas

Here are some ideas from the "Make" tasks in the chapters of this book. You might like to use one of them for the Project, but feel free to do something completely different. The only requirement is that it images part of the salvation story.

| Chapter | Theme | "Make" task |
|---------|-------|-------------|
| 1 | Creation | Tile-painting. Naming poem |
| 2 | Crisis | Word-twisting. Tile pieces |
| 3 | Calling | YHWH lettering/engraving. "The Call" prose/poem |
| 4 | Conception | Visual/written response to: the Annunciation, nurturing in the dark, finding an Elizabeth, the Magnificat or labor |
| 5 | Coming | Empty out your pockets |
| 6 | Cross and Comeback | Individual mosaic or group Cross mosaic |
| 7 | Charisma | Re-naming people, communities, or places |
| 8 | Community | Breviary |
| 9 | Church | Stones. Photo collage |
| 10 | Consummation | Homecoming |

# Appendix 3

**Imaging the story: the exhibition**

The exhibition is an opportunity to show all the projects created during the course, to share any insights gained, and to enthuse others to form a new group to read *Imaging the Story* and take the course themselves. The following are guidelines for a smooth-running set-up which is as professional as possible. Each exhibition will be different, of course, but attention to detail allows the work to be viewed at its best.

### The team

It is recommended that a sub-set of the larger group takes responsibility for organizing the show. In addition to an overall organizer, it is useful to include a person who is responsible for publicity, another with practical skills, and someone with an eye for detail. *Several* pairs of extra hands are helpful on hanging day!

### When and where

- It is best if the exhibition takes place a few weeks after the course has ended, to allow work to be finished and prepared for hanging, and in order not to lose momentum.
- As the *Imaging the Story* course progresses begin to consider possible venues that would be suitable. It could be your church, cafe, or local hall, or community center. Consider whether the natural light source is sufficient to see all the work well and decide whether extra lighting

is necessary, particularly if the exhibition will be viewed in the evenings. Think about access for all and car parking provision.

## Preparing the work

The exhibition is non-selective so each person should submit one piece (possibly two) by a *clearly communicated deadline date*. Work should be prepared for hanging once the method (see below) has been chosen and communicated.

## Hanging the work

- Allow *two days* for the hanging to allow for the unexpected.
- *Free standing painted boards* (hired or borrowed) create a clean gallery-style space that is easy and safe to move around, and offers maximum surface area for hanging. For a secure hanging attach *mirror plate* fastenings to frames, one each side. (They can be painted with a touch of paint identical to the board, if necessary.) In historic settings, if permitted, a sturdy hook is useful over an existing rim.
- For a *creative and economical approach to displaying*, see the images below where tables, staging, and cord are used.
- *Plinths* are tall Perspex or wooden boxes (painted white or the same color as the boards) on which sculpture or other 3-D work may be displayed.
- *White wall space* is good for projected work, but take extra care to cover all electricity cables.
- *Lighting* makes all the difference to viewing. Consider which pieces need natural light and use windows to best effect. Beware of reflections onto glass frames, and if additional lighting is needed use small LED clip-on spotlights.
- *Foam board* is suitable for displaying written work. Make sure everything is printed on white paper (letter size/A4) in the same sized font (14) and style (e.g., Times New Roman) to give a uniform appearance. Use a good quality spray adhesive to attach the paper to the foam board. Trim the work to size (after the glue has dried) on a cutting

board with a sharp craft knife. Use sticky fix adhesive pads to mount, having first checked that this is permitted.

- *Number labels* should be simple and clear and attached beside the work using a kind of adhesive that is permitted (extra attention is needed here in historic buildings). Foam board works well for this too, as is outlined in "Numbering the exhibits," below.

- Creating a simple catalogue or exhibition guide allows people to view the work in any order and it can be taken away and shared with others. List numbers on the left, followed by: the title of the piece, the name of the artist/author, the medium (e.g., oil on canvas, collage, watercolor), and a brief paragraph by the contributor highlighting processes, thoughts, inspiration, and the experience of making.

## Numbering the exhibits

- Type as many numbers as are required on white paper, font size 18, bold face, double spaced or more, to ensure there is enough space surrounding to place colored dots, should the work be for sale. It is a good idea to make a spare set in case of need!

- Cut numbers into strips the same width as the double-sided tape and stick strips to the foam board.

- Draw light pencil lines to divide the numbers or use the lines on a cutting board to guide for making shorter cuts.

- Cut out carefully with a craft knife on a cutting board and place into a container.

## Publicity

It's wise to get *promotional materials* designed and printed to give out on the last session of the course. These could be posters, postcards, fliers, images for church bulletins, and the creation of an event on social media. Include obvious information plus the time the presentations will begin.

Prepare any fliers for the next *Imaging the Story* course to give out at the end of the opening view.

## Opening view

Launching the exhibition can be a joyful occasion! It is a celebration of making, of friendships, and of accomplishment.

- Set a table in advance with drinks and canapés, and arrange for a few people to serve.

- Make exhibition guides available and encourage visitors to move around the exhibition using them. Also find an obvious place for them during the exhibition.

- Have some seats available for those who may not be comfortable standing once the presentations begin.

- After forty-five minutes or so gather people together and give a short introduction to the *Imaging the Story* exhibition, explaining the course, highlighting one or two themes.

- Invite as many people who wish to, to speak briefly about their work. Some might like to read any poetry/prose aloud. It is helpful to give a specific time limit and to arrange a signal to finish.

- The presenter can conclude this part by encouraging conversations and giving out fliers for the next course.

# Appendix 4

## Leader's guide

This course works best if it has a leader to guide the sessions. Ideally, two people will lead the group to provide a sounding board for each other and to help set up each session and to clear away. The groups can vary in size: we would recommend between twelve and thirty participants in order to have sufficient work for the exhibition, but the course can work with a smaller group.

Allow one-and-a-half to two hours for each session and have tea/coffee available. Do emphasize that before coming to a session it is essential that people read the relevant chapter and reflect on it. You will need to communicate with your group before the first session and tell them to read the introduction and chapter 1 (Creation). Have available a range of natural objects such as shells, leaves, or fruit, for drawing in the group session.

Give yourselves time as leaders to set up the room before participants arrive, particularly for any creative tasks that you will be doing in groups.

## Session outline

Each session should comprise the following:

### 1. Opening

Be intentional about the way you gather participants at the start of a session. People will have often come from busy weeks and will appreciate a chance to stop. You may like to start with a prayer, a piece of music,[1] or an image such as Gormley's *Sound II* (see the introduction) as a way of helping people to still themselves.

Give opportunity for people to behold the biblical text and the visual art and poetry during the session. Wherever possible, have the biblical text read aloud, as well as any poetry or prose pieces. Show the images from the chapter to the whole group. Receiving these pieces in a group context is a very different experience to reading/seeing them alone and may allow for new discoveries.

## 2. Group discussion

Give people the chance to share their experiences from the sections entitled "Read" and "Respond" in the chapters. You might like to split into smaller groups for this. Encourage people to share what they felt God was speaking to them about, particularly regarding creativity and the imagination, rather than simply giving an intellectual analysis of the material. Open-ended questions will leave more space for a range of responses. For example:

- How did you experience God as you responded creatively to the passage?

- What fresh insights did you gain from the "Make" task? In what ways were you stretched?

## 3. Make tasks

A. Leaders will need to provide the materials for the "Make" tasks that are to be done in the sessions.[2] These materials should be laid out before the activity and tables and chairs set up to accommodate groups of four to six working together.

B. Spend some time explaining the activity and invite questions for clarification before people start. You might like to show an example from the *Imaging the Story* website.

---

1  Be sensitive to the different church traditions (and none) that participants may be coming from.

2  These materials should be factored into the price of the course.

C. Leave 60–80 minutes for these tasks. Leaders will need to be on hand to help individuals and will not, therefore, have time to do the task themselves during the session. You might like to have background music playing while people are making, or you may prefer silence.

D. People will finish at different stages. Encourage early finishers to spend time on one of the other reflections from the chapter or to work on the Project (See Appendix 2).

## 4. Closing

Ensure that you leave time to share your work at the end, either around the tables or in the larger group. It is good to close with a prayer or a blessing at the end. Remind people to bring any materials they might need for the next session.

## Adapting the course to the church calendar

This material has worked well as a Lent course, with participants meeting weekly during the forty day period after Ash Wednesday and leading up to Easter. Exploring the salvation story through the lens of the arts can help people (re-)discover the wonder of the cross during Lent. Leaders will need to omit some chapters in order to do this; the remaining chapters could perhaps be tackled after Easter, leading up to Pentecost, or run as a Lent course the following year.

The following guidelines are designed to help the leaders to prepare for each session.

## Chapter 1: Creation

### Make

*Painted tiles*

The "Make" task for this session is continued in chapters 2 and 6. As leader(s) you need to make a decision about which activity to choose. The group can either make the "Mosaic Cross" or the "Individual Mosaic." Please *now* read the leaders' guide for chapter 6 "Make" details. You will need different paints in session 1 depending on the choice you make. If you decide to do "Mosaic Cross" be aware that at the end of this session you must collect *one tile* from every person (the second tile can be taken home). For "Individual Mosaic" collect *two tiles* from every person.

## Materials

- Have paper available, but encourage people to bring sketch books to each group session from now on
- Pencils
- Two smooth white ceramic tiles per person, approximately 15 cm or 6 inches square (they can often be found as surplus in hardware stores, often at no cost)
- Paints: (for *mosaic cross*) acrylic paints in red, blue, yellow, and gold, and white OR (for *individual mosaics*) ceramic/glass paints such as "Pebeo Porcelaine Paints"
- Paintbrushes and a selection of sponge brushes
- Paper or plastic plates for palettes
- Water pots
- Paper towels
- Protective table covers

## Instructions

- On paper sketch in detail something you see in creation. Draw on your memory, imagination, photos, or, alternatively, take a short walk outside. You may do two if you wish.
- From your loose sketches now distil the essence from your image, rather like Henri Matisse's cut-outs. What forms are you choosing to emphasize or exaggerate? Think about pattern and design.
- Paint your designs onto two white tiles and leave to dry. If using ceramic paints your leaders will heat fix the paint as per instructions.

*Leaders, don't forget to collect one tile from each person at the end. You will need to bring these tiles to the next session.*

## Chapter 2: Crisis

## Materials

*Word-twisting task*

- Long strips of paper (colored or white)
- Colored pens

*De-creative task*

- One tile per participant
- Protective gloves
- Safety glasses
- A tool with which to smash the tiles
- A protective container in which to smash the tiles (e.g. oil drum)
- An old blanket or sheet to protect the floor (if necessary)

## Make I

Discuss the relevant sections in chapter 2 ("Crisis") and complete the "Make" task in the chapter, exploring how God's words get twisted. Hang the word-twisting strips together.

## Make II

This second activity does not appear in the chapter but is pivotal to the course. As we follow the contours of the salvation story, you will now lead the group in a de-creative task to gain a glimpse into God's heart as sin mars his creation.

You should have kept a painted tile from each participant from the last session. Pass the tiles out, *ensuring that participants receive a tile that is not their own.* These are the instructions that should be given:

1. Look at the tile that someone else has made. Notice the choice of design and color behind it. What does it seem to echo of God's own enjoyment of making?

2. One at a time, go outside with the tile. Using a tool, smash the tile into small pieces (gloves and safety glasses are advised). Take your time.

3. Bring some of the fragments back and hold them before God in prayer. You might like to consider the fragments with regard to yourself, creation, your relationships with other people, and your relationship with God. As you hold the fragments, name the broken pieces in your own life and in this world honestly before God. You might want to write some of these things on the back of the tile fragments. Ask God's forgiveness for the way we have fragmented his beautiful world.

4. Give a few tile pieces to your group leader. Keep some for yourself.

## Discuss

- What did you experience as you smashed each other's tiles?
- What glimpse have you gained into God's sorrow at the fragmentary impact of sin on his creation?

## Music

If your group likes classical music, the smashing of the tiles could be done to Béla Bartók's *Duos for Two Violins*, Henry Purcell's *Golden Sonata*, or the last movement of J. S. Bach's *Concerto for Two Violins*.

## Important!

Leaders will need to keep the broken tile pieces safe (a few remnants from each participant) and bring them to Session 6.

## Chapter 3: Calling

### Materials

- Flower seeds
- Paper and pen

At the start of this session, take time to look back to the tile-breaking that took place in the previous session. Introduce the theme of calling and invite ideas as to how God calls us into his redemption purposes. Discuss how the arts might form a part of this.

### Vocation

Discuss in groups the answers to the questions at the end of each of the following sections in chapter 3:

- What makes you glad?
- What makes you sad?
- What makes you mad?

### Seeds of promise

Hand out some flower seeds. First, encourage participants to hold the seeds in their hands and to use their senses to explore them. What do they notice about them? How promising do they look? How much control do we have over what happens to them?

Next, give participants time to discuss their responses to Questions 1–4 in the "Seeds of promise" section (gifts being cultivated; gifts lying dormant; gifts I don't have; gifts that have come to fruition).

Finish this section with a prayer. Have participants choose a few seeds to represent the above answers and to hold them before God. Give thanks for God's promises fulfilled and for those seeds yet to reach fruition. Ask participants to hold onto some of their seeds for the next chapter—"Conception."

YHWH

Encourage the group to share what they made (wrote/engraved etc) with the name "YHWH." Pray that he would do the calling and that his name would underwrite all that they do.

## Make—"the call"

Invite participants to write their own poems or prose pieces to describe a call from God. You might want to give the following instructions:

*Visualize where you might be asleep creatively. Locate yourself in a scene—e.g., drifting off at your desk, dozing by the fire, etc. Jot something down to describe that place of slumber.*

1. *Now prayerfully imagine that God comes to wake you up, or sends someone to do so. How does he/she call you? What do they say? Note down anything you feel God asks you to do. You might like to look back through this chapter to see what God has been stirring in you already.*

2. *What are your feelings in response to this call?*

3. *Imagine the moment when you step outside. What kind of world awaits you? How do you feel upon entering it?*

4. *Write a prose piece or poem to capture this call from God.*

## Important!

Remind participants to bring some of their flower seeds to the next session.

## Chapter 4: Conception

### Materials

- Flower seeds
- Plant pots
- Potting compost/soil

## The Annunciation

After reading the passage, look at Filippo Lippi's *Annunciation* painting and discuss which "state" he seems to have caught Mary in.

### An open eye

Lippi draws on medieval optical theories, but the painting can still resonate for us today. Discuss these questions:

- What can we glean from this Renaissance notion of seeing? What might the metaphor of the "open eye" suggest about our relationship with God?

- John Drury suggests that Mary plays "noble host" to God's conception in her. Think about specific people and places you encounter. What might it look like to approach them with a hospitable gaze, as if receiving Christ himself?

- Are there areas in your life where you need to protect your seeing? You might want to think about what you expose your eyes to on the internet, television, films, and through print media. How might the tradition of the *hortus conclusus* be helpful here?

### Saying "Yes"—seeds

In the last chapter participants were asked to keep hold of some seeds to represent God's calling on their life. In this session they will sow the seeds in a pot. (Bring spare seeds along in case!)

Give time for participants to come individually and to sow the seeds in a pot. Look at what has been sown and turn this into a prayer, using Mary's words: "I am the Lord's servant. May your word to me be fulfilled" (Luke 1:38).

### Finding an Elizabeth

As a group, discuss any "Elizabeths" that people have in their lives. Who is helping you carry God's conceptions to term? Discuss the idea of "nurturing in the dark" and "bringing into the light" with regard to creative conceptions.

## Make

Encourage participants to share what they have started making in response to one aspect of the conception story (if they feel ready to bring it to light). Give them time to finish working on this during the session and then come back together to look at what people have made.

## The Project

Leave time at the end of this session to introduce the Project (Appendix 2) and to answer any questions. Try to ensure that each of the chapters in this book has at least one person covering it. Participants are free to contribute more than one piece of work, providing there is enough exhibition space. Encourage participants to meet in small groups as they plan and draft ideas and to chat to you. As a leader, you will be taking on something of an "Elizabeth" role.

## Chapter 5: Coming

### Respond

During this session encourage the group to show and speak about what they did in response to the Colossians 1 reading. Allow twenty minutes for this, ensuring that all who wish to have had an opportunity to speak and for discussion to take place.

### Discuss

Invite brief discussion from these sections of the chapter, particularly eliciting reflection on the beginnings of projects and word and image.

### Make

Before the session begins set up tables and chairs in a studio setting and protect the tables. The group will bring all they need to set up their collections of objects in a still life. Read the instructions from the chapter and clarify the task by inviting questions. Encourage the group to look carefully at shapes and the spaces in-between and to simply have a go. Allow an hour for this activity and leave room for the final reflection.

## Chapter 6: Cross and Comeback

Make

Choose *either* the individual mosaic *or* the cross mosaic tasks below and follow the corresponding instructions.

*Individual mosaic*

MATERIALS

- Paper and pencils
- Water pots
- Paper towels
- Soft sponges and rags
- Protective table covers
- Plastic spoons and knives
- ¾ inch or 2 cm plywood cut into 8 inch or 20 cm squares, one per student
- Tile grout
- Tile adhesive

Figure 58

**Figure 59**

**Figure 60**

INSTRUCTIONS

- Draw round the wooden base and thoughtfully arrange the broken tiles in a design, working from the outside to the center.
- Spread tile adhesive onto the base and carefully transfer the fragments onto it working in the same way as above.
- Spread tile grout over the design, ensuring all the spaces are filled, then remove the excess.
- Gently wipe with a damp sponge and clean further with a rag till all grout is removed from the mosaic. Set aside to dry thoroughly.

*Mosaic Cross*

**Figure 61**

MATERIALS

- 1/16 inch or 2 mm thick acrylic sheet available from a D.I.Y. store.
- Decorator's plain lining paper
- Straight edge metal ruler
- Craft knife
- Fine sandpaper
- 2" or 3" x 1" timber
- An equivalent amount of cup hooks as acrylic strips
- A drill
- Several glue guns

**Figure 62**

INSTRUCTIONS

For full details and pictures on how to make the mosaic cross please see www.imagingthestory.com.[3] Making this cross is a reflective/worshipful activity during which people select tile fragments and stick them onto acrylic strips, guided by a cross shape on paper beneath. This is a group activity.

3   Our grateful thanks to Stephen Owen for designing this process (http://www. stephenowen.com/wood.htm)

## Chapter 7: Charisma

### Images of the Spirit

Look at the different images used to point to the work of the Spirit in the Bible (bird, wind, fire, etc). Spend some time looking at William Blake's *Sketch of the Trinity*. Discuss which images resonate most with participants and elicit their experiences of the Holy Spirit.

### Breathe on us

### Reflect

As a group, encourage participants to bring their creative "charisms" and to lay them before God. They can do this physically, bringing their sketchpads, notebooks, laptops, or any other creative tools, and laying them down. They could also bring any work they are preparing for the exhibition project. Look again at Blake's *Sketch of the Trinity*. Invite the Holy Spirit to brood over each stage of your making—from the conception of the idea, through to its planning and execution, and finally, to its birth—and to equip you all with skills for each stage.

Ask the Holy Spirit to breathe on each of you so that you "image the story." You might like to turn Edward Thomas's poem in chapter 7 into a prayer.

### "The ministry of re-imagination"

Discuss the idea of "re-naming" people, places, and situations according to the way God sees them. Elicit examples.

### Make

Participants continue what they started with the "re-naming" task in this chapter.

Just as the Holy Spirit gifts us with *charisms*, people should feel free to give away what they make in this session. Pray God's blessing on them as they go out.

## Chapter 8: Community

Making a bréviary

*Materials per person:*

Make sure that the following are available and set out on tables before the group arrives. Feel free to add any other materials you have available. As you launch this task underscore that approaching prayer in this way is exploratory and may not appeal to everyone. Emphasize the multi-sensory aspects that aim to prompt prayer, but also ensure that people don't feel guilty about missing certain "hours" or become legalistic about the activity! Encourage open-minds and willingness to have a go. Let the group know that there will be an opportunity to share their experience of praying this way during the next session.

- Eight strips per person of colored card or heavy white watercolor paper that has been loosely hand-painted in various shades (approx. 0.8 inches x 4 inches or 2 cm x 10 cm)
- Scissors
- A piece of ribbon or cord, (6–8 inches or 15-20 cm in length)
- Medium-sized beads
- Colored pens
- A one-hole punch

*Instructions*

Use the details from chapter 8.


## Chapter 9: Church

Rhythmic prayer

Invite feedback on the experience of praying the "hours" during the past week.

- To what extent were they able to keep the prayer routine?
- What effect did repetition have on their prayers?

- Did they encounter God differently? If so, how?
- Which scriptures stood out, why?

## Haiku

Invite the group to share the Haiku poems they wrote, if they wish. If there are several groups you may wish to ask for permission to print them and share them in written form.

## Reviewing the project

Set a positive tone for discussion about the project. Some will be well on the way, others less so. The questions in "Reflect" on the passage allow everyone to give a status report. Initially, do this in pairs and then broaden out to the whole group for a brief update. Be prepared to encourage and to offer sensitive guidance as it is requested.

## Make

If someone in the group is planning a project for the church, let them share initial ideas and invite discussion to explore the idea more fully. If this is not the case, let the group choose together from one of the following ideas (or add your own) and prepare a case study based on the suggestions in the chapter.

- Make an appropriate participatory activity for a Good Friday service as part of a traditional three-hour liturgy.
- Design an aspect of a Christmas festival that seeks to defamiliarize the nativity and engage those beyond the church.
- Create a collaborative piece with and for children based on the life and work of a particular saint.
- Devise a short reflective service for the bereaved with a sensitive participatory dimension.

## Chapter 10: Consummation

### The eagle's view

Linking back to John's "eagle's" perspective in the introduction, discuss the visual threads of the salvation story that are finally consummated in Revelation 21–22. Spend time looking at Roger Wagner's stained glass window, *The Flowering Tree* (St. Mary the Virgin Church, Iffley, UK). It would be good to provide digital access also during this session to Michael Takeo Magruder's *De/coding the Apocalypse* exhibition.

Discuss how our making might help people "Come further up, come further in" to the ending of this story. Look at *Coming Home* by Ros Mansfield and elicit any responses to the "Reflect" section. Read the quotation from Lawrence Thornton's novel and discuss how the arts can help us to dwell inside God's imagination while we wait for Christ's return.

## Make

Invite participants to share the drafts or ideas for their own "homecoming" pieces and give them time to "dream" on their own during the session. Alternatively, they might prefer to work on the Project, either individually or in groups.

You might like to use the Tom Wright's quotation from "Jesus, the Cross and the Power of God" as a commission before you close this last session.

On a practical note, make sure everyone knows what he or she needs to do for the exhibition!

## Appendix 5: Further commentary on artists and artworks

### Chapter 6: Cross and Comeback

**ECLAT AND RÉFLÉCHIE, 2015 (91CM X 130CM), ACRYLIC ON BOARD BY GILL C. SAKAKINI (WWW.GILLSAKAKINI.COM)**

The grounds of these two panel paintings evoke the enclosed garden or *hortus conclusus* in which Mary is often depicted in medieval iconography.

The garden typically delineates the space in which Mary's purity is protected from the world and has echoes of the garden in the Song of Songs. A devotional reading is not necessarily intended here; rather the bold botanic design of the wallpaper (reminiscent of 1970's French style) is a vehicle for emphasizing Mary's emotional interior space. The brush strokes, colors, and fleshly treatment of Mary emphasize her humanity and are reminiscent of her depiction as a robust young woman working in the weaving process in third-century Egyptian Annunciations.

*Eclat* captures a contemporary *post*-Annunciation moment in which the teenage Mary, alone in her room, responds to Gabriel's news through a bursting, embodied "YES!" The "garden," like creation itself, shares the immediacy of her joy through the shape of wide open, fully ripe petals, which reinforce the openness of her limbs in this accepting gesture.

Reading from left to right a visual pilgrimage takes place in the space between the paintings. In *Réfléchie* the petals of the garden ground are now dried seed pods pointing to the necessity of the seed of Christ falling to the ground and dying to make way for new life. Mary is once again solitary, this time caught in a moment of reflection after the presentation of Jesus at the temple to Simeon and Anna. In contrast to *Eclat*, Mary's body folds inwards, creating a small space, and her gaze is directed to the right, to the light source, as she reflects on Simeon's prophecy that "a sword will pierce through your own soul also."

Taken together these paintings ask questions through gesture, viewpoint, pattern, and color about the tension of holding conflicting things together, such as messiahship and death, joy and sorrow, keeping and letting go.

## THE EARTHQUAKE AND THE ASCENSION BY RICHARD CAEMMERER.
### FROM THE STATIONS OF THE RESURRECTION 2010, IN ST. MARY'S CHURCH, OLD BASING AND LYCHPIT, HAMPSHIRE, ENGLAND (WWW.RRCSTUDIOS.COM)

Richard was cofounder of the Grünewald Guild, WA, and his work can be found in church, museums, and private collections all over the world.

*THE CROSS AND COMMUNION TABLE* BY STEPHEN OWEN.
AT GUILDFORD BAPTIST CHURCH, MILLMEAD, GUILDFORD,
SURREY, ENGLAND (WWW.STEPHENOWEN.COM)

The table communicates that death does not have the last word in the Gospels. Based on the empty tomb, the communion table is a visual reminder of those words, "He is not here—He is risen!" The base of the table is made from one solid piece of 120-year-old green oak and will therefore move (shake) with time, reminding us that the tomb could not contain the risen Christ. At one end of the base, the center of the original tree can be seen. The rough surface at the bottom gives way to a smooth, tapered top; a symbol to us as we take communion that Christ was the perfect sacrifice, once for all.

In making the cross-shaped lectern, the artist wished to bring attention back to the immediacy and reality of the cross. The large nail driven through the lectern's base is a sharp reminder of the sacrifice Jesus paid for us at Calvary. The crossbeam indicates the open pages of the word of God. The texture of the wood changes from rough to smooth as the eye moves up the piece, reflecting God at work in us, transforming us from "one degree of glory to another." At the bottom there are slits in the wood into which written prayers can be tucked.

## Chapter 8: Community

*SYRIAN BROTHER AND SISTER* BY HANNAH ROSE THOMAS
(WWW.HANNAHROSETHOMAS.COM)

This young artist paints portraits of people she encounters on her travels, from African women in remote villages in Mozambique to Syrian refugees in Jordanian refugee camps. She has painted while volunteering in the Calais "Jungle" in France. Her intimate portraits seek to humanize individuals forced to flee their homes, whose personal stories are otherwise shrouded by statistics. She draws inspiration from Islamic art and Arabic poetry, to celebrate the rich heritage of the Middle East, so often forgotten and overshadowed by war. Hannah is currently studying for an MA at the Prince's School for Traditional Arts, London.

## Chapter 9: Church

The making of this piece incorporated two distinct elements of the textile-dyeing process: one predictable and one exploratory. For example, real stones (physical matter) were secured into white fabric to make background marks and the second part of the process was left open-ended. The whole was hand-dyed in yellow ochre Procion™ dye with the predictable result of subtle organic or fossilized forms. Meanwhile, to form the stones, black cotton fabric was wound around a length of plastic pipe and ruched at intervals with string. Household bleach was dribbled from the top and penetrated the fibers in an arbitrary way.

After neutralizing in a water and vinegar solution, the unfolded fabric revealed surprising pale pink fibrous patterns, which resembled human tissue on a microscope slide! The fabric was cut into stone shapes and adhered to the ochre ground to resemble a cairn, a way marker, as a picture of the church as guide and indicator of the path.

## Chapter 10: Consummation

***Coming Home*** by Ros Mansfield
(www.soulspacepilgrimage.co.uk)

My painting is about
the kiss,
the embrace
when a mother holds her child,
when Mary held Christ,
and as Christ embraces creation.

The space that is created
Is a space of safety for your soul.
The outside world can't come in . . .
It is a returning to where one is most at peace,
and held.
Both ancient and modern.

# Bibliography

Alter, Robert. *The Five Books of Moses: A Translation with Commentary*. London: Norton, 2004.

Anselm. *The Prayers and Meditations of St. Anselm with the Proslogion*. London: Penguin, 1973.

Arts. *The Arts in Religious and Theological Studies* 25.1 (2013) New Brighton.

Athanasius of Alexandria. *On the Incarnation: The Treatise De Incarnatione Verbi Dei*, New York: St. Vladimir's Seminary, 1998.

Avis, Paul. *God and the Creative Imagination: Metaphor, Symbol and Myth in Religion and Theology*. London: Routledge, 1999.

Baker, Heidi. *Birthing the Miraculous*. Lake Mary, FL: Charisma House, 2014.

Barth, Karl. *Church Dogmatics* iii, pt. 3. Translated by G. W. Bromiley and R. J. Ehrlich. Edinburgh: T. & T. Clark, 1960.

Baxandall, Michael. *Painting and Experience in Fifteenth Century Italy*. 2nd ed. Oxford: Oxford University Press, 1988.

Begbie, Jeremy, ed. *Beholding the Glory: Incarnation through the Arts*. Grand Rapids: Baker, 2001.

Bell, Rob. "Beginning in the Beginning." On *Poets, Prophets and Preachers*. Seminar DVD. Grand Rapids, July 2009.

Benner, Juliet. *Contemplative Vision: A Guide to Christian Art and Prayer*. Downers Grove, IL: IVP, 2011.

Bennett, Sarah. "An Artistic Response to the Trafficking of Isan Women in Bangkok as Prostitutes." BA hons. thesis, Belmont University, Nashville, TN, 2008.

Berkhof, Hendrikus. *The Doctrine of the Holy Spirit*. Richmond, VA: John Knox, 1964.

Blake, Quentin. "Drawn into a Parallel World." *The Daily Telegraph Review*, May 25, 2013, R28. Article following a talk at the Hay Festival.

Bonhoeffer, Dietrich. *Life Together*. London: SCM. 1954.

Brand, Hilary, and Adrienne Chaplin. *Art & Soul: Signposts for Christians in the Arts*. Carlisle, UK: Piquant, 2001.

Brown, David, and Ann Loades. *Christ: The Sacramental Word*. London: SPCK, 1996.

Brown, Rosalind. *Being a Deacon Today: Exploring a Distinctive Ministry in the Church and in the World*. Norwich, UK: Canterbury, 2005.

Brueggemann, Walter. *The Creative Word*. Philadelphia: Fortress, 1982.

———. *Finally Comes the Poet: Daring Speech for Proclamation*. Minneapolis: Augsburg Fortress, 1989.

———. *Genesis: Interpretation: A Bible Commentary for Teaching and Preaching*. Atlanta: John Knox, 1982.

———. *Hopeful Imagination: Prophetic Voices in Exile*. London: SCM, 1986.

———. *The Prophetic Imagination*. 2nd ed. Minneapolis: Fortress, 2001.

Bryson, Norman. *Looking at the Overlooked: Four Essays on Still Life Painting*. London: Reaktion, 1990.

Buechner, Frederick. *Wishful Thinking*. San Fransisco: Harper San Fransisco, 1993.

Burgess, Katherine. "Our Lady of Perpetual Exhaustion." *Washington Post*, 24 September 2013. Online: https://www.washingtonpost.com/national/on-faith/our -lady-of-perpetual-exhaustion-exhibit-probes-the-spirituality-of-everyday-chaos /2013/09/24/08bfc7c4-255b-11e3-9372-92606241ae9c_story.html.

Bustard, Ned. *Revealed: A Storybook Bible for Grown-Ups*. Baltimore: Square Halo, 2015.

Cavanaugh, William T. *Torture and Eucharist: Theology, Politics and the Body of Christ*. Oxford: Blackwell, 1998.

*Chariots of Fire*. Directed by Hugh Hudson. Warner Bros., Goldcrest Films, Allied Stars Ltd., The Ladd Company, 1981.

Chesterton, G. K. *Orthodoxy*. New York: Image, 1959.

Collicutt, Joanna. *The Psychology of Christian Character Formation*. London: SCM, 2015.

Corrie, John, and Cathy Ross, eds. *Mission in Context: Explorations Inspired by J. Andrew Kirk*. Farnham, UK: Ashgate, 2012.

Csikszentmihalyi, Mihaly. *Flow: The Psychology of Optimal Experience*. New York: Harper Collins, 1990.

Daly, E., and L. Moffat, eds. *Contemporary Art in British Churches*. London: Art and Christianity Enquiry, 2010.

Davis, W. V. *R. S. Thomas: Poetry and Theology*. Waco, TX: Baylor University Press, 2007.

Deuck, Ryan. "The Plot We Find Ourselves In." January 7, 2016. Online: https:// wonderingfair.com/2016/01/07/the-plot-we-find-ourselves-in/.

Dewar, Francis. *Invitations: God's Calling for Everyone*. London: SPCK, 1996.

Drury, John. *Painting the Word: Christian Paintings and their Meanings*. New Haven and London: Yale University Press, 1999.

Dyrness, William, ed. *The Christian Imagination*. Image Journal 15 (1996). Online: http:// imagejournal.org/product/issue-15/.

Eisner, Elliot W. *The Arts and the Creation of Mind*. London: Yale University Press, 2002.

Eldredge, John. *The Journey of Desire*. Nashville: Thomas Nelson, 2000.

Epiphany. *Sound Portraits*. Online: http://epiphanymusic.org.uk/sound-portraits.

Fiddes, Paul. *Participating in God: A Pastoral Doctrine of the Trinity*. London: Darton, Longman and Todd, 2000.

Freedman, Linda. *Emily Dickinson and the Religious Imagination*. Cambridge: Cambridge University Press, 2011.

Giles, Richard. *Here I am: Reflections on the Ordained Life*. Norwich, UK: Canterbury, 2006.

Goan, Chris, ed. *Learning to Love*. PROOST Poetry Collection 1. Available as a PDF from www.proost.co.uk, 2014.

Greenslade, Philip. *The Big Story: Revealing God's Covenant Plan for Everyone*. Farnham, UK: CWR, 2001.

———. *A Passion for God's Story*. Carlisle, UK: Paternoster, 2002.

Grün, OSB, Anselm. *Benedict of Nursia: His Message for Today*. Collegeville, MN: Liturgical, 2006.

Guinness, Os. *The Call*. Carlisle, UK: Paternoster, 1998.

Guthrie, Steven. *Creator Spirit: The Holy Spirit and the Art of Becoming Human*. Grand Rapids: Baker Academic, 2011.

Haynes, Deborah. "The Place of Art." In *Arts, Theology, and the Church: New Intersections*, 158–76. Cleveland, OH: Pilgrim, 2005.

Heaney, Seamus, trans. "The Names of the Hare," anonymous Middle English lyric. From *Opened Ground: Poems 1966–1996*, 209–10. London: Faber and Faber, 2013.

Heschel, Abraham. *Moral Grandeur and Spiritual Audacity: Essays*. New York: Farrar, Straus and Giroux, 1996.

Hopkins, Gerard Manley. "God's Grandeur." In *Gerard Manley Hopkins: The Major Works*, 128. Oxford: Oxford University Press, 2002.

House, Paul. "Outrageous Demonstrations of Grace." In *Great is Thy Faithfulness?* edited by Robin Parry and Heath Thomas, 26–52. Eugene, OR: Pickwick, 2011.

Jacobs, Alan. *Original Sin: A Cultural History*. London: SPCK, 2008.

Jensen, Robin M. *The Substance of Things Seen: Art, Faith, and the Christian Community*. Grand Rapids: Eerdmans, 2004.

Jensen, Robin M., and K. J. Vrundy, eds. *Visual Theology: Forming and Transforming the Community through the Arts*. Collegeville, MN: Liturgical, 2009.

John Paul II. "The Creator Spirit and Artistic Inspiration." From *Letter of John Paul II to artists*. Online: https://w2.vatican.va/content/john-paul-ii/en/letters/1999/documents/hf_jp-ii_let_23041999_artists.html.

Joynes, Christine E., ed. *Perspectives on the Passion: Encountering the Bible through the Arts*. London: T. & T. Clark, 2007.

Kelly, Gerard. *Spoken Worship: Living Words for Personal and Public Prayer*. Grand Rapids: Zondervan, 2007.

Laing, R. D. *The Divided Self*. London: Penguin, 1960.

Lawrence, Michael. *Biblical Theology in the Life of the Church: A Guide for Ministry*. Wheaton, IL: Crossway, 2010.

Levertov, Denise. *New Selected Poems*. Hexham, UK: Bloodaxe, 2003.

Lewin, Ann. "Revelation." In *Watching for the Kingfisher*, 122. Peterborough, UK: Inspire, 2004.

Lewis, C. S. *The Last Battle*. The Chronicles of Narnia, Book 7. London: Harper Collins, 1956.

———. *The Screwtape Letters*. London: Bles, 1942.

———. *Surprised by Joy*. London: Fount, 1955.

Martin, Paul, ed. *Making Space for Creativity*. Brighton, UK: University of Brighton, 2010.

McElroy, J. Scott. *Creative Church Handbook: Releasing the Power of the Arts in Your Congregation*. Downers Grove, IL: IVP, 2015.

McIntyre, John. *Faith, Theology and Imagination*. Edinburgh: Handsel, 1987.

———. *The Shape of Pneumatology*. London: T. & T. Clark, 1997.

Meyers, Carol. *Rediscovering Eve: Ancient Israelite Women in Context*. Oxford: Oxford University Press, 2013.

Milburn, Robert. *Early Christian Art and Architecture*. Berkeley: University of California Press, 1988.

Misopolinou, Anna. *Ecstasy: A Source of Intimacy or Applications of the Dionysiac Model for Grotowski's Theatre*. Online: http://people.brunel.ac.uk.

Morley, Janet. *The Heart's Time*. London: SPCK, 2011.

Muir, Edwin. "The Annunciation." In *Collected Poems*, 223–24. London: Faber and Faber, 1960.

Nichols, Aidan. *The Art of God Incarnate*, London: Darton, Longman and Todd, 1980.

Nouwen, Henri J. M. *The Only Necessary Thing: Living a Prayerful Life*. Edited by Wendy Greer. London: Darton, Longman and Todd, 2000.

Novak, Michael. *Business as a Calling*. New York: Simon and Schuster, 1996.

O'Hear, Natasha. *Contrasting Images of the Book of Revelation in Late Medieval and Early Modern Art*. Oxford: Oxford University Press, 2011.

Ortberg, John. *If You Want to Walk on Water, You've Got to Get Out of the Boat*. Grand Rapids: Zondervan, 2001.

Paintner, Christine Valters. *Eyes of the Heart: Photography as a Christian Contemplative Practice*. Notre Dame, IN: Sorin, 2013.

Pattison, Stephen. *Seeing Things: Deepening Relations with Visual Artefacts*. London: SCM, 2007.

Peterson, Eugene H. *Christ Plays in Ten Thousand Places*. Grand Rapids: Eerdmans, 2005.

———. *The Message: The Bible in Contemporary Language*. Colorado Springs: NavPress, 2002.

———. *Tell it Slant: A Conversation on the Language of Jesus in his Stories and Prayers*. Grand Rapids: Eerdmans, 2012.

Pickstock, Catherine. "What Shines Between: The *Metaxu* of Light." In *Between System and Poetics*, edited by T. Kelly, 112–18. Aldershot, UK: Ashgate, 2007.

Powell Jones, T. *Creative Learning in Perspective*. London: London University Press, 1972.

Pritchard, John. *The Life and Work of a Priest*. London: SPCK, 2007.

Quash, Ben. *Found Theology*. London: Bloomsbury, 2013.

Rees-Larcombe, Jennifer. *A Year's Journey with God*. London: Hodder and Stoughton, 2010.

Richardson, Jan. *Circle of Grace: A Book of Blessings for the Seasons*. Orlando, FL: Wanton Godspeller, 2015.

Robinson, Marilynne. "The Deeper Mind." Interview in *Poets and Writers*, Nov/Dec 2015, 36–43.

Schakel, Peter, ed. *The Longing for a Form: Essays on the Fiction of C. S. Lewis*. Kent, OH: The Kent State University Press, 1977.

Seed, eL. "A Project of Peace Painted across 50 Buildings." TED talk, 19th July, 2016. https://www.ted.com/speakers/el_seed.

Sherry, Patrick. *Images of Redemption: Art, Literature, and Salvation*. London: T. & T. Clark, 2003.

Siegel, Lee. "Where Have All the Muses Gone?" *Wall Street Journal*, May 16, 2009. Online: www.wsj.com/articles/SB124242927020125473.

Simmons Roberts, Michael. *Corpus*. London: Cape Poetry, 2004.

Sink, Susan. *The Art of the Saint John's Bible: A Reader's Guide to Historical Books, Letters and Revelation*. Collegeville, MN: Liturgical, 2012.

Soupiset, Paul. "The Labyrinth Project." Lentenblog, April 2008. Online: http://soupiest. typepad.com/soupablog/the_labyrinth_project.

Stackhouse, Ian. "Crisis." In *Seeing His Story*. Lent Course by Gill Sakakini and Karen Case-Green, Guildford, 2014.

———. *The Day is Yours: Slow Spirituality in a Fast-Moving World*. Milton Keynes, UK: Paternoster, 2008.

Steinberg, Leo. "'How Shall This Be?' Reflections on Filippo Lippi's 'Annunciation' in London," Part I. *Artibus et Historiae* 8.16 (1987) 25–44.

Strati, Antonio. *The Aesthetic Approach in Organization Studies. The Aesthetics of Organization.* Edited by S. Linstead and H. Höpfl. London: Sage, 2000.

Takeo Magruder, Michael. *A New Jerusalem* [artwork], 2014. Online: http://www.takeo.org/nspace/2014-dta-new-jerusalem/.

Taylor, Barbara Brown. *The Preaching Life: Living Out Your Vocation.* London: Canterbury, 2013.

Taylor, V. John. *The Go-Between God.* London: SCM, 1972.

Taylor, W. David O. *For the Beauty of the Church: Casting a Vision for the Arts.* Grand Rapids: Baker, 2010.

Thomas, Edward. "Words." In *The Collected Poems of Edward Thomas,* edited by R. Thomas, 71–73. Oxford: Oxford University Press, 1978.

Tomlin, Graham. *Looking through the Cross.* London: Bloomsbury Continuum, 2014.

———. *The Widening Circle: Priesthood as God's Way of Blessing the World.* London: SPCK, 2014.

Viladesau, Richard. *The Beauty of the Cross: The Passion of Christ in Theology and the Arts—From the Catacombs to the Eve of the Renaissance.* Oxford: Oxford University Press, 2006.

Volf, Miroslav. *Free of Charge: Giving and Forgiving in a Culture Stripped of Grace.* Grand Rapids: Zondervan, 2005.

Vrundy, Kimberly, and Wilson Yates, eds. *Arts, Theology, and the Church: New Intersections.* Cleveland, OH: Pilgrim, 2005.

Williams, Peter S. "Apologetics in 3D: Persuading across Spiritualities with the Apostle Paul." 2013. Online: http://www.bethinking.org/apologetics/apologetics-in-3d.

Williams, Rowan. "The Frontiers of Poetry." 1977. Online: www.sagepublications.com.

Wright, N. T. *The Challenge of Jesus.* London: SPCK, 2000.

———. "Jesus, the Cross and the Power of God." Conference paper presented at European Leaders' Conference, Warsaw, February, 2006.

———. *Luke for Everyone.* London: SPCK, 2001.

Yancey, Philip. *Grace Notes.* Grand Rapids: Zondervan, 2009.

———. *Vanishing Grace.* London: Hodder and Stoughton, 2014.

Printed in Great Britain
by Amazon